YOUR TOWNS & CITIES IN WO

DARLINGTON AND TEESDALE

AT WAR 1939–45

For my parents

YOUR TOWNS & CITIES IN WORLD WAR TWO

DARLINGTON AND TEESDALE

AT WAR 1939–45

CRAIG ARMSTRONG

Pen & Sword

MILITARY

AN IMPRINT OF PEN & SWORD BOOKS LTD.
YORKSHIRE - PHILADELPHIA

First published in Great Britain in 2022 by
Pen & Sword Military
an imprint of
Pen & Sword Books Ltd
Yorkshire – Philadelphia

ISBN 978 1 52670 480 1

A CIP catalogue record for this book is
available from the British Library.

Typeset by SJmagic DESIGN SERVICES, India.
Printed and bound in the UK by CPI Group (UK) Ltd.

Pen & Sword Books Limited incorporates the imprints of Atlas, Archaeology,
Aviation, Discovery, Family History, Fiction, History, Maritime, Military, Military
Classics, Politics, Select, Transport, True Crime, Air World, Frontline Publishing,
Leo Cooper, Remember When, Seaforth Publishing, The Praetorian Press,
Wharncliffe Local History, Wharncliffe Transport, Wharncliffe True Crime and
White Owl.

For a complete list of Pen & Sword titles please contact
PEN & SWORD BOOKS LIMITED
47 Church Street, Barnsley, South Yorkshire, S70 2AS, England
E-mail: enquiries@pen-and-sword.co.uk
Website: www.pen-and-sword.co.uk

Or
PEN AND SWORD BOOKS
1950 Lawrence Rd, Havertown, PA 19083, USA
E-mail: Uspen-and-sword@casematepublishers.com
Website: www.penandswordbooks.com

Contents

CHAPTER 1

Organising the Home Front

Air Raid Precautions, Home Guard and other Groups

During the summer of 1939, with war obviously now coming, Darlington's ARP scheme was fully mobilised. The preparations were very rushed, however. The day before war was declared, the town's ARP headquarters, in the basement of the public library on Crown Street, was established and workers sandbagged the basement windows. The coming conflict was obvious elsewhere in the town too. Workers were busily sandbagging various public buildings, while work was hastily progressing with the air raid trenches. Despite the attempts of the authorities, however, there was still a shortage of labour, and an appeal for volunteers to aid in the sandbagging of Darlington Memorial Hospital and the various first-aid posts was put out. Dr G.A. Dawson, the town's medical officer, also appealed for male volunteers to form stretcher parties and first-aid parties at the Baths Hall, Dodmire and North Road Schools.

This was reflective of the fact that, despite the war now being certain, the ARP and civil defence services still did not have enough volunteers in their ranks. A particular problem, not just in Darlington but across the North, was a lack of recruits to the Auxiliary Territorial Service (ATS). In particular, female typists, telephonists, and cooks were in short supply and volunteers were urgently requested to come forward.

The ARP services were not the only organisation desperately trying to get new recruits. The local Territorials were also advertising a large number of vacancies in the days before war was declared. On 1 September an advert for volunteers for the Darlington Territorials appeared in the *Daily Gazette for Middlesbrough*. There was a particularly urgent need for fitters and instrument mechanics who would service and repair anti-aircraft guns and instruments. There were more limited vacancies available for electricians, turners, welders, coppersmiths, blacksmiths, wheelwrights and motor drivers. Clearly the majority of these vacancies were in specialised roles and were suitable only for skilled workers.

The outbreak of war may not have brought the immediate air raids which were feared by many of the British people, but the preparations for such attacks continued unabated. The various Air Raid Precautions (ARP) organisations were arranged by specially appointed ARP committees on local councils. Darlington was no different. Councillor R.F. Scott was appointed as Darlington's ARP Controller. The task of the controller was an exceptionally difficult and complex one. The controller was responsible not only for the overall coordination, equipping and operation of the complicated ARP scheme for the town, but also expected to promote the activities of ARP organisations and to ensure that adequate numbers of people were available for the services. The vast majority of those who served in the various ARP

Advert for Darlington Territorials. (Daily Gazette for Middlesbrough)

organisations were volunteers while others were drawn from council employees. Whilst the ARP organisation of the town was most visible through the air raid wardens, it also included light and heavy rescue squads, decontamination and gas squads, first aiders, salvagers, those working to rehome and feed those who had been bombed out, and others. A great number of administrative workers, cooks, telephonists and drivers were also needed for the various services. The highly visible wardens were often an unwelcome presence who were seen as interfering busybodies. Councillor Scott appears to have been well aware of this difficulty and had initiated an ARP Information Bureau which would disseminate information about the work of the ARP organisations. Although preparations had been in place for many months, in some places since 1937, the actual mobilisation of the services brought myriad problems.

In Darlington, one of the early and more troubling problems reflected not only the difficulties faced by the authorities, but also a concerning lack of patriotism among some of the local business communities. Just days after the declaration of war, Councillor Scott wrote to the local press claiming that he had become aware of several incidents where employers had made it difficult for employees who had volunteered for ARP service, while others had put measures in place which made it impossible for employees to volunteer and to retain their jobs. Councillor Scott relayed one incident in which an employee had approached his employer and notified them of his responsibilities to national service, only to be immediately told that his services were no longer required. This was, of course, completely unacceptable and Councillor Scott entreated anyone encountering such difficulties to contact him immediately and reassured volunteers that steps would be taken to remedy the situation.

Despite such problems, the first week of the war saw something of a rush of volunteers to join the ARP services in Darlington. The first seven days of the war saw 1,423 people enrol in ARP services in the town. This brought the total number of ARP personnel in Darlington to between 4,000 and 5,000. Wednesday, 6 September was the most popular day for recruitment with some 818 people volunteering. Although the eagerness to serve was encouraging, many vacancies remained, with shortages of volunteers to be stretcher bearers particularly acute.

One of the most important hubs in the ARP network was the ARP Report Centre which was responsible for the coordination of the ARP scheme in the event of raiding. The realities of the war, however, meant that certain men who had been given key positions in the ARP scheme suddenly found that they had more duties than they could cope with. Darlington's ARP organisation suffered an early setback when Superintendent H. Huitson, the man who had been given charge of the report centre, resigned after discovering that his additional police duties meant that he could not fulfil his duty in the ARP scheme. He was replaced by the principal of Darlington Grammar School, Dr A. Hare.

Despite the plans which had been put in place to both assist and control the civilian population in the event of emergency, the authorities also had to ready themselves for enforcement action in the event of citizens who failed to rise to the occasion. Although the authorities expected people to pull together, there was clearly some doubt, and those in authority believed that some people would try to exploit the wartime situation; one of the concerns was that people might attempt to secure extra supplies of coal or coke by submitting fictitious amounts of their yearly usage. The provisional fuel overseer, borough librarian Mr F. Dallimore, informed the ARP Information Bureau and the local press that such a practice would not be successful because the amounts registered on application cards were to be cross-checked with the books of the local coal merchants.

Clearly the Darlington authorities recognised the necessity of keeping people as informed as possible and the creation of the ARP Information Bureau was one aspect of this. Another was the creation of a citizen's advice bureau which would coordinate the work of local social service organisations. The bureau occupied a prominent place in the town next door to the enrolment room for the Women's Voluntary Service (WVS).

The somewhat ramshackle approach to some preparations even extended to the supply of gas-mask respirators. Everyone should have been issued with a respirator before war was declared, but there were worrying problems in Darlington. As late as 12 September, the press were reporting that some people in the town did not have a respirator, despite the fact that it was illegal to go out without one, and that the only source of the respirators – the ARP station at Houndgate – had run out. The initial supply for the town had been exhausted in the first week of the war and a further supply of 750 respirators had been distributed on 9 September. Although it was hoped that more adult respirators would shortly be available, the town had yet to receive any supplies of babies' helmet respirators.

Organising the various ARP groups was a monumental task and the realities of war led to some dislocation of the pre-war planning. Vital to the successful running of the ARP services were key appointments of those in charge of the force, but many suitable candidates already had many other duties or were called up for other wartime service.

By the end of September 1939 the authorities in Darlington were still making appointments to important ARP and civil defence positions. A meeting was scheduled for 27 September at which the position of Mr F. Dallimore, who had been acting as provisional fuel overseer, was confirmed, along with that of fuel controller; appointments to an advisory committee were also discussed. Clearly this indicates a certain lack of preparedness among the local authorities which would have an impact upon the effectiveness of the local scheme. Another prime concern was that the civilian population would be required to produce far more of its own food to take the burden off the already stretched supply lines across the Atlantic. Thus, the Darlington Corporation's Streets Committee discussed the probability that there would be a demand made for the expansion of the number of allotment plots within the town. The result of the meeting was that the borough surveyor, Mr E. Minors, was tasked with locating suitable sites within the town and to subsequently report to the Allotments Sub-Committee.

By 1940 the ARP and civil defence services in Darlington and Teesdale had been granted sufficient time to bed-in and the organisation of the various services was a large improvement on that which had existed at the beginning of the war. For many, however, the organisations were increasingly being viewed with some scorn as the war failed to develop as people had anticipated. The lack of wartime action also meant that the attitudes of many people towards precautionary measures were changing; something which greatly concerned the authorities.

Although the Phoney War was continuing in France and there was some laxity among the people of Darlington, the authorities in charge of the town's ARP services were determined that the men and women of the service would be as well prepared as possible. On Sunday, 28 April, the largest exercise yet held in the town involved every section of the ARP services. It was hoped that the exercise would enable more training but would also be of benefit in making each section of the ARP services more aware of, and better coordinated with, the others. The exercise involved faked incidents using volunteers as casualties and not only included the ARP services but also the local police and fire services along with the hospitals. The exercise simulated a full-scale attack on the town and included mock incidents where people were trapped, a chemical incident and a thorough workout of the first-aid and medical services using the simulated casualties. Afterwards, special demonstration squads drawn from the various services were to give demonstrations of their techniques to other ARP services and to the public.

Despite the determination of the authorities to maintain a spirit of caution among the general populace, the ARP services in the Darlington area were not seriously tested during 1940. Raiding over the area was very sporadic and no large raids targeted the town specifically. There were a number of minor incidents in which the ARP service could hone its skills. In the early hours of 27 August 1940, for example, some bombs fell on Port Clarence. Damage was slight but such minor incidents provided much needed practice for the ARP organisation.[1] This incident was followed just over a week later when bombs fell on Darlington in the early hours of 5 September. Minor damage and fires were started and there was one injury but further lessons were learned, including the fact that the water supply in some of the more rural areas was lacking. Several bombs fell on a farm on the outskirts of the town and a haystack and outbuildings were destroyed by fire because the fire brigade had no access to water.

Although 1940 passed reasonably quietly for Darlington's ARP services, this in no way limited the amount of strain or lowered the workload for those who were tasked with running the organisation. Those members of the council who had found themselves undertaking ARP duties had been forced to work extremely hard in order to pull together the force and to make sure it was trained and equipped, and maintained its sense of morale in order to undertake its duties in the event of an air raid. The chairman of the ARP Emergency Committee and ARP Controller, Councillor R.F. Scott, was recognised in the New Year's Honours list for his contribution to both local government – he had been a member of the council since 1933 – and to the ARP scheme in Darlington, where he had been committee chair since 1937, with the award of an OBE.

For many men who were not involved in the ARP services and who had not been called up for service there was often a sense of helplessness, lack of purpose and even, in some cases, shame that they were not playing what they considered to be an active role in the war. Many former soldiers in particular were eager to be more actively involved. There had been a great deal of pressure placed upon the government by various groups lobbying on behalf of these men. The pressure had begun shortly after the start of the war, but the situation was exacerbated by the loss of France and the threat of invasion, and the government capitulated and, in May 1940, asked for men to volunteer for the Local Defence Volunteers (LDV). It was at first envisioned that this force would have a very restricted and minor role, and the number of volunteers was expected to be modest.

However, by noon on the day following the announcement of the formation of the LDV, more than 100 Darlington men had put their names forward and recruitment continued apace. The men were from a broad section of society and trades and professions. They included a banker, butchers, electricians, plumbers and a chauffeur. The vast majority were middle-aged men, many of whom had served in the First World War. When speaking to the press these men said that they believed the LDV was essential for the defence of the country and that they thought it was time to step forward and serve. One consequence of the enthusiasm was that some men who were already serving in the ARP services now wished to join the LDV, seeing it as a more active contribution to the defence of the country. Darlington's ARP Controller, Councillor R.F. Scott, quickly moved to clarify the rules, telling ARP workers that only if their role was part-time could they put their names forward for the LDV.

The enthusiasm for the LDV was not solely related to Darlington, and across all of the towns and villages of Teesdale the scenes of men trooping to police stations was repeated. In many of the more rural areas men quickly organised themselves into sections and, arming themselves with shotguns and whatever else could be found, set about patrolling within days.

The initial recruitment and organisation of the LDV was rather haphazard and marred by disorganisation. The local police stations, which had not been pre-warned, were quickly overwhelmed by the number of men who came forward to give their details and local organisation of the force in Darlington, as elsewhere, was largely a purely local initiative. The authorities in Darlington were keen to placate the volunteers and, although describing the response as 'overwhelming' and admitting that not every volunteer had been contacted a week after the appeal had gone out, told the press that many volunteers had already been enrolled and that further volunteers were still coming forward. The people of Darlington, it claimed, could 'be assured that the job is being efficiently done'.[2]

This keenness to instil confidence was heightened by the fact that Darlington had an initial key role in the LDV organisation for the whole Northumbrian Command Area which included the North Riding of Yorkshire, County Durham and Northumberland. The headquarters of the Northumbrian Command Area was based in Darlington at the time and the officers attached to this HQ had a very busy time as they were largely responsible for seeing that the LDV in the area was well organised and that it liaised with the regular forces. Each county in the command area was divided into groups and each group divided into companies, platoons, and sections. One of the biggest problems facing the LDV was the lack of suitable weaponry and equipment. In Darlington the LDV were boosted by the early issuance of a small quantity of rifles, ammunition and clothing. Uniforms, however, were not available and so they had to make do with armbands bearing the letters LDV.

Among the men who came forward for the LDV were a large number of cyclists and, with a key duty of the force being reconnaissance and communication, these volunteers were quickly organised into cyclist sections at Stockton on 22 May 1940. This response was despite the fact that many cyclists had already volunteered to serve as ARP messengers. The recruitment of cyclists in the Teeside LDV force also highlighted the friction which quickly came to define the relationship between the volunteers and the government. The LDV in the area urged young female cyclists to consider offering their services as parachute landing scouts with local organisers as this was considered suitable work for young women. This was contrary to government instructions which stated that the LDV would be a male only force.

Although the LDV – soon to be renamed the Home Guard at Churchill's urging – quickly established itself, the lack of arms, ammunition and uniforms proved a constant source of irritation to many of its members. Another growing concern was the fact that many came to believe the government was backtracking on some of its promises and that the role envisioned for the force was too passive. Despite these concerns the Home Guard continued to train and to slowly equip itself.

With the Home Guard still actively recruiting throughout 1941, many men were placed in something of a quandary because they wished to join and serve, but realised that their full-time jobs were also vital. A number of Darlington teachers had expressed their wishes to be permitted to sign up. The Board of Education informed the Home Guard that teachers would be permitted to join as the Home Guard was a voluntary part-time force.

The ARP services were also still recruiting and the need for fire-watchers was of particular concern to many industrial premises. Mid-January 1941, for example, saw adverts in the press for a number of vacancies at Darlington Forge Ltd. Four full-time men were required for roof-spotting duties in connection with the works' ARP organisation: there were ten full-time vacancies for firefighters in the works' firefighting service (the applicants were to have some general ARP experience and preference was given to men who had firefighting experience), and there was a vacancy for a works' security officer who had military experience as he would be expected to deal with the works' Home Guard unit.

The Home Guard might have been viewed with derision in some quarters, but the vast majority of the force were determined and as well-trained as possible given the circumstances. The presence of so many semi-trained men and firearms did, however, lead to tragedies. Such a case was heard at Darlington in late August of 1941. Earlier in the month several Home Guard units were engaged in a shooting competition. A platoon from Leyburn were shooting at the time of this particular incident. The platoon sergeant, George Parsley, was pulling back the cocking-piece of his miniature rifle when he slipped and the rifle went off. Another member of the platoon described how he had heard the shot followed by a cry of 'I have been shot.' George Miles Lumley (31) had been struck in the foot by the bullet and subsequently died. Sergeant Parsley stated that he had 'known Lumley since he was a boy and they were great friends'. The coroner at Darlington, Mr J.E. Brown-Humes, returned a verdict of accidental death and stated that 'This man died in the service of his country as much as if he had been on active service.'[3]

While the common view of the Home Guard is coloured by the immensely popular *Dad's Army* TV show, with the perception being that the force was made up of old men, the average age of men was, in fact, the mid- to late 30s. Many were men in their 40s who had served in the First World War, while other younger members worked in reserved occupations. There were, however, examples which fitted in nicely with the stereotype. The oldest member of the Darlington Home Guard was Mr Thomas Emerson of Bracken Road. On 2 September Mr Emerson celebrated his 84th birthday. This determined octogenarian was a former schoolmaster who had retired in 1922. He and a dozen other veteran members of the Home Guard provided a 12-hour continuous guard at Home Guard Headquarters and carried out duties such as answering the phones and receiving callers. Each man took a three-hour turn at this duty. Another veteran member of the Darlington Home Guard was Mr John Hugill, an international clay pigeon shot who had competed for England against the other Home nations.

Earlier in the war Darlington's Civil Defence Controller had visited his counterpart at Nottingham, and in late June 1943 there was a reciprocal visit when the controller at Nottingham visited to inspect the town's civil defence cooking arrangements, stores, first-aid posts, vehicle repair shops and so on. One of the things that linked the two services was that they both had a highly efficient messenger service which was assisted by the Civil Defence Cadet Corps. The Nottingham controller inspected this force and was delighted by what he saw. He finished his visit by attending the Civil Defence Cadet Corps quiz which was held at the Scout Hall.

By 1944 it was becoming more obvious that the need for the Home Guard was passing, but the men of the force still continued to serve and played a substantial role in maintaining morale. For one Darlington Home Guard platoon, 17 May 1944 brought some welcome relief from their sterner duties. The soldier son of the platoon's officer was getting married and the NCOs and men of the platoon formed a uniformed guard of honour for the happy couple. The bridegroom was Sergeant Joseph Scott of the Royal Electrical and Mechanical Engineers (REME) and his bride was Miss Joan Boyd.

The ARP services remained at their duties in 1944, but this year also brought great changes at the head of the organisation. In early 1944 a crisis gripped nearby Newcastle upon Tyne when a government inquiry into alleged corruption within that city's ARP and civil defence organisations resulted in several scathing criticisms and subsequent resignations. As a result of this inquiry the government issued new guidance to local authorities regarding those people who should be employed at the head of such services. One of the recommendations was that no one should hold a position in the civil defence services that was incompatible with membership of the local authority's Emergency Committee, which oversaw the administration of the service. As a result, the head of Darlington's civil defence organisation, Councillor Scott, tendered his resignation from his chairmanship of the Emergency Committee. The resignation was accepted but, keenly aware of the situation in Newcastle, the council made it known that it had been accepted with regret and the General Purposes Committee placed on record its appreciation of his service and their entire confidence in him. Indeed, Councillor A.J. Alsop said that in his opinion, Darlington had been 'very much favoured in having a man of the calibre, ability and courage of Councillor Scott at the head of its Civil Defence organisation'.[4] During the meeting at which Councillor Scott's resignation was accepted, Councillor Alsop stated that Scott had devoted the whole of his time to his duties and Alsop was pleased that Scott was to remain as head of civil defence. Fulsome tributes were also paid by Alderman A.J. Best, Alderman J.D. Hicks, Councillor R. Luck and the Mayor, Councillor A. Trees.

Although the Home Guard in 1944 was obviously just a short period away from being wound down the men still went about their duties. Given the often arduous physical nature of these duties it was almost inevitable that there would be some casualties. The Darlington Home Guard suffered a particularly sad loss in October 1944 when Lieutenant Stanley Arthur Morgan, aged 46, died of natural causes. Mr Morgan worked as a fish and game dealer and lived at Salutation Road. Like many of the Home Guard he had served in the First World War, with the Royal Artillery. Mr Morgan left behind a widow and a son who was serving with the Royal Armoured Corps.

Just a month after the death of Lieutenant Morgan the Home Guard was stood-down. This was a very sad occasion for many members. Those who had joined in the earliest days, when Britain was threatened with invasion, believed that they had given valuable service and, for many who had served in the previous war, the force provided a sense of comradeship which had not been experienced since their earlier service days. It was announced that a stand-down parade would take place on 3 December with the salute being taken by the commanding officer, Lieutenant Colonel S. Riley Lord. The parade would be followed by farewell speeches at the Drill Hall.

Following on from the stand-down of the Home Guard, tributes were paid to the officers of the 20th (Darlington) Battalion. Two silver candlesticks and a silver salver were presented to Lieutenant Colonel Riley Lord by Colonel C.E. Vickery, MP, while the second-in-command, Major A.B. Leake, received a silver cigarette case. Silver spoons were presented to Captain W.F. Dunne, adjutant, and a silver salver to Captain F.R. Robson, quartermaster. The presentation ceremony was presided over by Major Robert Desmond Ropner. A grandson of Sir (Emil Hugo Oscar) Robert Roper, Baronet of Preston Hall and Skutterskelfe Hall,

Major Ropner was also the brother of Conservative MP Leonard Ropner. The Ropner family had formed extensive shipbuilding and shipping businesses in the local area and the family were extremely influential.

December also brought the announcement of the award of a British Empire Medal to one of the most useful members of the Home Guard in Darlington. Sergeant Henry W. Johnson was a member of 'E' Company, 20th Battalion, Durham (Darlington) Home Guard and had acted as a musketry instructor to many of the local Home Guard companies. He was a Bisley marksman and had won many international honours for his marksmanship. He had also been the secretary of the Darlington LNER Rifle Club for twenty years. Mr Johnson lived at Banklands Road and was a turner at the Darlington LNER Works.

With the Home Guard having been stood down there was, for some, a sense of loss. Many Home Guardsmen, especially those older members who had found a sense of comfort in the comradeship engendered by serving in the force, were unwilling to let that go in the event of disbandment. In Darlington, the 20th Battalion obtained War Office approval to form the 20th Battalion, Durham (Darlington) Home Guard Rifle Club. The aims of the club were 'to keep alive some of the associations formed during training days of the Home Guard',[5] and by 13 April 1945 the club already had 300 members signed up and was planning its first 'shoot' on 22 April at the Neasham range. The club was also expected to arrange an extensive plan of social activities for its members.

CHAPTER 2

Wartime Life

The reality of the war meant that, as a part of the ARP preparations, there was a rush to fortify important locations in Darlington. One of the duties to which troops, both Regular and Territorial, were put to in the first days of the war was in assisting both the military and civilian authorities in providing protection from air raids in the form of sandbagging. Many troops spent the first days of the conflict filling sandbags which were to be used to protect local sites and to fortify military defences and air raid shelters. This duty brought an early wartime tragedy to Darlington.

On 5 September 1939 troops from the Territorial 50th (Northern) Division Signals, Royal Corps of Signals, were at work with some local workmen in a quarry at Barton, filling sandbags when there was a landslip. As the lip of the quarry gave way, the other workers heard a crash and cries for help. They immediately dashed forward and one man, Mr R. Abbott, even managed to briefly grab the hand of a soldier before he was buried. The rescuers were then forced back by a second slip which completely buried five soldiers. Mr Abbott related how he had reached the scene of the collapse and had seen one soldier up to his shoulders in sand and that the soldiers had been completely buried by the second landslip, which buried Mr Abbot himself up to his neck. He was quickly rescued when word was spread, and the entire neighbourhood turned out to help. They were assisted by 100 workers from a nearby sandpit. The task they faced was huge with the soldiers being buried under 100 tons of sand and soil.

Two soldiers were dug out within minutes and were largely uninjured, but the three missing men were not recovered until over one hour later; the three young Territorials were dead. Signalman Joseph Hinnigan (26) was a Darlington native and had lived in Belgrave Street with his wife of three years, Euphemia Lillian Hinnigan. He also left behind his parents, James and Charlotte. Signalman Sidney Case (20) was originally from Gateshead but he and his parents had moved to Darlington several years earlier, and lived at Salisbury Terrace. The Case family had connections with the Darlington area and the dead soldier was a cousin of a well-known Darlington amateur boxer. The final fatality was Signalman George William Treslove (17). Another Darlington native, Signalman Treslove left behind his parents John and Eliza of Harrowgate Hill, Darlington.[1]

It was a day of accidents in Darlington although, thankfully, the two other accidents did not result in such tragedy. Bank worker Kenneth Law was fixing up blackout blinds above the glass roof of the National Provincial Bank on High Row when he slipped and fell. Mr Law crashed through the glass roof and his body fell some 25ft to the floor of the bank. During the fall he struck several metal bars with such force that they were bent and he landed next to a typist. Mr Law was taken to hospital by ambulance, but miraculously was allowed home after treatment to his back and ankle. The other accident took place at the Cleveland Bridge and Engineering Company premises when Mr George Bradley (61) of Falmer Road suffered a fall in the timber shop. Mr Bradley was taken for treatment at Darlington Memorial Hospital but was allowed home after treatment.

One of the most immediate changes to the lives of people in Darlington was the enforcement of the strict blackout regulations. Just days after the declaration of war the local magistrates made it clear that they were determined to enforce the regulations sternly. Alderman J.D. Hinks commented to the local press that Darlington had a good record but that there was still room for improvement in some areas. He expressed the belief that lapses were due more to carelessness than to indifference, but he asked that 'the public pay full attention to the restrictions'.[2]

Along with the new ARP and blackout restrictions there was also a great deal of concern over what aspects of civilian life would be seriously impacted by the war. One of the areas in which there was immediate uncertainty was sports. With large crowds forbidden to gather, and certain restrictions placed in many areas which were seen as being vulnerable or protected as militarily vital (especially the east coast), many sporting bodies were thrown into confusion. The football authorities in the Northeast, for example, were left with the knowledge that they would probably only be allowed to play friendly fixtures – but even this was not certain. The situation was made even more uncertain when a list of places where matches could not be played was published. It included Newcastle-upon-Tyne, Tynemouth, Wallsend, South Shields, Middlesbrough, Sunderland, West Hartlepool, Hartlepool, Jarrow, Felling, Hebburn, and Whickham. The Durham Football Association revealed on 9 September that it had received no official guidance or information from the English FA, but that it understood that spectators who were not carrying respirators would be turned away from friendly matches by police. It was also understood that all matches would be friendlies, but that 'Victory' leagues might be formed later, as had happened during the First World War.

A meeting of the board of directors of Darlington FC was held on 11 September, but little new information was available. Chairman Mr J.B. Smith stated that if the ban on competitive football was lifted, then it was possible that regional leagues may be instituted. There were obvious difficulties for the Northeast, however, as so many locations were on the list of places where matches could not be played due to government restrictions.

There was another unavoidable accident on 12 September 1939 which claimed the life of an elderly man on Croft Bank. Mr Albert Jennings, a retired engineer who lived at the Temperance Hotel, Croft, was sitting on a roadside seat, reading, when a 2-ton military lorry approached. The driver, Alfred Nicholson, related to the subsequent inquest that he had just turned a corner at the top of the bank and was doing approximately 20 mph when the steering suddenly gave way without any warning and the lorry careered out of control, striking Mr Jennings. The elderly man was taken to Darlington Memorial Hospital with serious injuries but died of shock. The jury concurred that Nicholson could not have done anything to avoid the incident and a verdict of accidental death was returned.

With the war at the forefront or everyone's minds, it was also recognised that entertainment was necessary to relieve some of the tensions. At first there had been consternation when the government had announced that all theatres and cinemas were to be closed, but it was quickly realised what a mistake this was and the decision was reversed. Cinemas across Darlington were permitted to reopen from 9 September, although they were to close at 10pm. The cinemas maintained their huge popularity during these first days and weeks of the war with Darlington being no different. Theatres and halls also provided much-needed relief. In mid-September Darlington's New Hippodrome at Parkgate was offering what it described as a 'bright, fast-paced variety show' which, despite the difficulties of wartime travel restrictions was 'well up to usual standards'. The show featured sketches, musical turns, and 'up-to-date dancing acts by a first-rate cast'.[3] A week after this show, the New Hippodrome was advertising a more topical variety show entitled 'Take Cover', featuring the northern comedian Frank E. Franks among others, and the management promised that 'Even National Service workers will be bound to laugh when they see the funny side of A.R.P. as presented by the top cast.'[4]

As the war progressed, the exigencies of wartime existence often meant that opportunities for entertainment were limited. With many workers in Darlington factories and works having to work extra hours in demanding jobs and with the stresses of wartime living, there was a movement to allow cinemas and theatres to have Sunday matinee performances. The owner of several cinemas across the North, and of a theatre in Darlington, Mr E.J. Hinge, supported this proposal as he believed it would be welcome relaxation for those workers who had no opportunity of attending through the week. Mr Hinge stated that for such workers, the only opportunity at the moment was the Saturday matinee; this resulted in overcrowding and many people having to be turned away. The overcrowding was compounded by the attendance of many people who did not wish to risk the journey in the blackout.

Others sought comfort and relief from tension in more traditional ways and church attendances in Darlington increased at the beginning of the war. The popular evensong services, however, were impacted by the added dangers of the blackout and many Darlington churches decided to move the evensong services to a less dangerous time in the afternoon.

The lack of immediate aerial attack led to some people taking a more relaxed attitude towards the carrying of gas-masks. These respirators were meant to be carried at all times but their unpopularity, combined with the lack of immediate attack, had caused some laxity among the Darlington populace. A survey conducted late in September 1939 found that of fifty-four pedestrians who passed the junction of Parkgate and Tubwell Row, only sixteen were carrying their respirators. It had been impossible to determine if three were carrying their respirators or not, but the figure of more than two-thirds not obeying the official instructions was worrying for the authorities. In an effort to ensure that civilians did carry the respirators, Darlington Corporation made it a condition of boarding Darlington trams and buses, but it seemed that many people were carrying empty cardboard respirator boxes or were making their own paper mache boxes in order to board the buses. One of the comic-strips in the local press even gently mocked the phenomenon of carrying a fake respirator box in order to access public transport.

By October 1939 some sports were returning, albeit in the form of friendly matches. Darlington RFC took on an Army XV at Hundens Lane at the beginning of the month in a match which was somewhat overshadowed by the recent death of a member of the club. The match finished in a 28-0 victory for Darlington with their greater pace proving

Comic-strip mocking false respirator box carriers. (Northeastern Gazette)

the difference. The club, however, was in mourning for Pilot Officer John Scott, who had been killed in a road accident on 6 October. Pilot Officer Scott had been in the RAF for two years but had only recently earned his wings. His body was discovered beside his motorbike at 5.30am on the morning of 6 October and an inquest determined that he had suffered his death as a result of coming off his machine at Maltby Lane Ends near Yarm during the blackout. Pilot Officer Scott was serving with 608 (North Riding) Squadron. The Auxiliary Air Force squadron was, at the time, flying Avro Ansons with RAF Coastal Command from its base at Thornaby. Just days after their defeat by Darlington RFC the Army XV took on and defeated Darlington RA by 18-6 at the Brinkburn Road ground.

Since the institution of the blackout there had been a number of fatal road accidents, and the overall number of accidents had increased hugely. Another fatal accident occurred on the night of 19 October when Mr Gilbert Dent (34) of Hundens Lane, Darlington, was struck by a car and a trolley-bus. The inquest into Mr Dent's death revealed that Mr Dent had not been cautious enough when crossing Woodland Road and had been struck first by a car and then by the trolley-bus which was immediately behind it. He suffered a fractured skull and was dead upon his arrival at Darlington Memorial Hospital. The coroner and jury absolved the drivers of any blame and the coroner added that Mr Dent did not appear to have taken the precautions that were the duty of every pedestrian when crossing the road in the blackout, adding that he did not wish to say anything harsh about Mr Dent as he had only done 'what hundreds of other people do every night of their lives, and if his death can in any way assist to bring home to the masses the danger, then you may think he did not altogether die in vain'.[5]

Pilot Officer John Scott. (Northeastern Gazette)

The blackout clamed yet more tragic victims when there was a terrible motor accident on the Great North Road near Chilton on the night of 27 December. A car collided head on with a lorry and one young man, Harold Musgrave (24), was killed outright while his brother, Stanley Richard Musgrave (20), their cousins, Alfred (23) and Flora Marks (21), and Stanley's friend, Cyril Ezra (20), were injured. Stanley, a medical student, succumbed to his injuries three days after the crash. Harold was buried at Darlington West Cemetery on 29 December and his brother was buried next to him on New Year's Day. Before the second funeral, which was conducted by the Rabbi to the Darlington Hebrew community, Rabbi S. Barron, the men's father, Maurice, commented that they had been devoted to each other in life and said that it 'was always their wish that they should never be parted. They were always together.'[6]

The spate of traffic accidents seemed to continue into February 1940. On 5 February a double-decker bus toppled over onto its side after it tried to avoid a collision with a lorry on the road between Darlington and Sadberge. Some of the bus passengers had lucky, even miraculous, escapes from the accident and none were seriously injured. The bus, owned and operated by United Automobile Services Ltd, was travelling around a bend on a narrow stretch of the road near to Darlington when the lorry, owned by Tarslag Ltd of Stockton, came into view. The bus driver, Stephen Dickinson, swung the bus to the left of the road but its near-side wheels mounted a high verge and the bus toppled. Part of the lorry was crushed by the bus but the driver, James Blackburn, scrambled free without injury, even though his cab had been crushed. Mr Dickinson was trapped in his cab but freed by rescuers. The bus, which was a regular service from Stockton to Darlington, had a number of passengers on board but many were able to leave by the escape door on the upper deck. A Sadberge man, Walter Thurston of 4 Norton Road, who witnessed the accident knew that his 14-year-old daughter, Hilda, was on board. He went to the aid of the passengers and was relieved to find that Hilda had suffered only minor injuries.

The beginning of December 1940 brought yet another inquest into the death of a young soldier who had been killed in a road accident. 23-year-old Gunner Michael Leonard of 409th Battery, 53 (5th Royal Northumberland Fusiliers) Searchlight Regiment, was riding a motorcycle at Keverstone Corner, near Staindrop, when he collided with a stationary bus. The Darlington inquest heard that it appeared that the young soldier lost control when he saw the bus in front of him. The Darlington coroner, Mr J.E. Brown-Humes, acquitted the bus driver of all blame and, recording a verdict of accidental death, added that the corner was undoubtedly a dangerous one and that he hoped the authorities would make some improvements to decrease the danger.[7]

The blackout was only one way in which the war had an early effect on the lives of civilians. While the war was a source of severe anxiety for many, for some young lads it brought a frisson of excitement to their lives and many were eager to join up for what they saw as the sheer adventure of serving during wartime.

On 21 December 1939, 16-year-old Malcolm Sanderson of Feethams, Darlington, set out on his bicycle for his workplace at the farm of his uncle, Mr J.K. Dods of Denton Hall, Piercebridge. The alarm was raised when Malcolm failed to arrive. Malcolm was described as looking older than his age and had previously expressed his desire to join the Army but had been forbidden from doing so by his mother who told him he was too young.

By the first week of January 1940 there was still no sign of the missing youth. Extensive inquiries had failed to find any trace of him, but a possible clue arose on 7 January when a motorist reported giving a lift to a boy whom he believed could have been the missing teenager. Mr H. Smeaton, the motorist concerned, informed police that on the morning the boy had gone missing he had given a lift to a lad whom he had earlier seen repairing a bicycle at the side of the road. He was wearing clothes similar to that which Malcolm had reportedly been wearing, and he had asked the way to Boroughbridge.

A day after the motorist had come forward, the police managed to trace the missing teenager. On the evening of 8 January he was found to be serving in the Army in Scotland. The police discovered that on the day after he had gone missing he had joined up at Leeds under his full name of Fred Malcolm Sanderson. Mrs Sanderson had spoken to Mr George Dugill, the son of Darlington's Mayor, who was studying in Scotland and he had confirmed that her son was with the Army in Edinburgh.

The presence of so many soldiers, sailors and airmen in the town, along with the blackout and the stresses of wartime Britain, caused some people to grow anxious about a possible decline in moral standards. At the start of March 1940 the Archdeacon of Durham, the Venerable E. DeV. Lucas, gave a speech at St Agnes Home, Darlington, in which he addressed the importance of moral welfare work in wartime. The Archdeacon was at pains to say that this was not because he believed that when men put on uniform they became monsters, and to say that the dangers of the presence of so many servicemen had been greatly exaggerated by some people. However, he added, many of these men were away from home and that made a great deal of difference as it resulted in 'a certain slackening of restraint, a certain temptation to be freer with the common decencies of life'; this was the reason why the work of groups such as St Agnes was so important. In replying to the Archdeacon, the secretary of St Agnes, Mrs Kent, commented on the fact that women patrols had been arranged with the cooperation of the police in an effort to maintain orderliness in the streets. In a rather less judgemental address, the Reverend H.G. Hastings-Shaddick, Rector of Haughton-le-Skerne, said he believed a great contribution could be made by the people of Darlington in giving a warm welcome to servicemen stationed in the town because many of them 'were from good homes and had left good jobs at the call of their country'.[8]

Without chivvying by the church authorities, some of the people of Darlington had already ensured that visiting servicemen would receive a warm welcome in the town. The beginning of the war had seen a large number of service clubs being speedily organised and opened. These clubs provided refreshments and other facilities to service personnel who found themselves travelling throughout the country. During the First World War a Soldier's Club had been set up at Darlington's St Cuthbert's Parochial Hall, just a five-minute walk from the town's Bank Top Station and proved immensely popular, with an estimated 57,000 passing through it during the course of the war. The club was quickly revived at the beginning of the Second World War, providing free beds for servicemen left stranded in the town, along with a meal at a nominal cost and writing facilities. It also provided weekly concerts for troops, which were held in the hall. The club once again proved its popularity with between 6,000–7,000 men having already taken advantage of its facilities throughout 1940. In March the club was featured in a broadcast on the forces radio show entitled 'In the Night Hours'; the work of the club was covered in some detail, along with testimony from servicemen who happened to be present at the time of the visit of the mobile broadcasting unit. One of the weekly concerts, featuring the 'Arptimist's Concert Party', a group made up entirely of ARP personnel, also made an appearance, along with an interview with Alderman W.G. Chandler, who had been a worker at the hall during the First World War and was working there again during the Second World War. Musical support was provided by several girls from the ATS; so successful were the girls that they were invited back to give a concert themselves. As a result, the girls formed their own concert party called the 'Depot Delights of 1940', and on the night of 3 April they made their first public appearance at the club in front of 400 uniformed members of the forces. The BBC broadcast was an unashamed propaganda effort which, it was hoped, would encourage the development of similar facilities throughout the country with the Darlington Soldiers' Club being held up as a fine example of what could be achieved.

Although the authorities were keen to maintain morale among the civilian population, the Ministry of Information was widely distrusted as so much of the information available was either not released to the public or was so heavily censored as to be useless, while some of the information released had later proved to be wrong. With the fall of France and with the British people being told that they were now alone (they were not, of course; this discounted the Empire) facing the Axis, there were some who were eager to demonstrate that there was still resistance in the occupied countries. On 25 April, Darlington Tea Club were entertained by a talk from Madam De la Courcelle, the wife of the General de Gaulle's civil representative to the north of England, on the evidence of resistance among the French people under occupation.

While the authorities focused on maintaining morale, some organisations seemed determined to continue as if nothing untoward had occurred anyway. Many cycling clubs took advantage of fair weather in May 1940 to hold outings. West Hartlepool Club had a large number of members for its ride on Sunday, 5 May 1940. The route was from Burn Valley through Wolviston and Sadberge to Croft Spa, where lunch was taken. The cyclists then proceeded via Scorton to Brompton-on-Swale where a pleasant afternoon was spent on the banks of the River Swale. The club then cycled home via Darlington.

Meanwhile, the Tees Valley Beagles held their annual meeting on 18 May. Mr C. Chipchase and Mrs S. Sadler, of Sadberge Hall, were elected joint-masters. It was noted at the meeting that costs for hound meal, etc, had increased to £16 and the hope was expressed that this would soon be alleviated by more people coming forward to walk the hounds.

The warm weather in early June 1940, combined with the number of children who were no longer in full-time education, would lead to disaster. At the beginning of June a 9-year-old boy named John Raymond Neasham, of Woodland Road, was paddling in the River Tees at the waterworks dam near Coniscliffe Road, when he slipped and fell into the water. Thirteen-year-old Alan Wilkinson was fishing nearby and saw the boy in the water. He tried to get John to grab the end of his fishing rod but was unable to do so. The brave young lad then partially stripped and jumped into the river to try to rescue John, but although he managed to reach him, he could not get a hold of the youngster and he went under the surface. Auxiliary fireman Albert Leeming (26) arrived on the scene and also got into the river to try to rescue the now submerged lad. Leeming discovered the boy lying on the bottom of the river and he was recovered with the use of a grappling iron. Mr Leeming applied artificial respiration, but the boy died. A coroner's hearing expressed admiration for the two who had attempted to rescue young John and added that the location was a dangerous one and urged parents to keep their children away from it.

For members of the Quaker movement, the war presented a dilemma. They were dedicated to peace but it was clear that the threat of Nazi Germany was a dire one. Many, faithful to their pacifist beliefs, refused to be called up or to serve and were classed as conscientious objectors. Forced to appear before the conscientious objector tribunals they were met with a variety of attitudes ranging from understanding and sympathy to outright hostility. Some, eager to do their bit while retaining their pacifist beliefs, volunteered for the medical services and some fifty or so from the local area volunteered to serve with the Red Cross 'Friends' Ambulance Unit which was being dispatched to Finland. One of the first two to arrive in Finland was a native of Darlington. The adjutant of the unit was Mr Alan R. Dickinson, a Darlington chartered accountant.[9]

With the war situation getting increasingly worse it is no surprise that there was little sympathy felt for those who registered themselves as conscientious objectors. On 4 June 1940 Darlington Town Council's General Purposes Committee, which consisted of all the members of the council sitting in private, voted through a motion that any employee of the corporation who, upon being called to register for military service, registered as a conscientious objector would be immediately given notice to terminate his service with the corporation. This draconian motion was passed by twenty votes to nine.

Throughout the year the people of Darlington had thrown their full support behind the men and women in the forces, and those who were on the front lines continued to receive marvellous support from the town in the form of charity fundraising and the donation of various comforts. It is no surprise that many people's minds also turned to the remembrance of past conflicts. With Armistice Day falling on Monday, 11 November 1940 and coinciding with market day in Darlington, the council were determined to ensure that a greater effort than usual was made; on 10 October a meeting took place at the Town Hall and arrangements were discussed. A stall in the market selling poppies was organised, along with several other stalls throughout the town and it was hoped that a shop would be made available as a central depot for the campaign. In 1939 the campaign had raised over £700 and it was hoped that this figure would be exceeded in 1940. Mr W. Ridyard, the president of the Darlington branch of the British Legion, took the opportunity to thank the outgoing Mayor for the interest he had taken in the Legion and in ex-servicemen during his tenure. The Mayor-elect, Councillor H. Wilcock, thanked the Mayor for his work and commented that he had been set a high standard to follow.

On 4 November 1940, the same day that they Mayor was opening a charity sale at the auction mart, the Deputy Mayor, Councillor A.J. Alsop, and the Mayoress were opening an exhibition of war photographs at the Darlington Public Library. The photographic collection had been provided by the Ministry of Information and covered every aspect of the war so far, including an extensive section on the London Blitz.

One of the biggest fundraising efforts of the year was the War Weapons Week which began on Saturday, 23 November 1940. The town hoped to raise the grand total of £650,000 for the cause. Traders were asked to decorate their premises with flags and patriotic bunting while the campaign would begin with the biggest procession the town had ever seen. Several bands took part and a naval contingent led the parade. A mechanised Army unit also took part along with representatives of the RAF, ATS, Home Guard and civil defence services. The newly-elected Mayor, Councillor Henry Wilcock, and the commanding officer of the Northumbrian area, Brigadier P.J. Shears, took the salute from a dais on High Row while the route of the parade was lined by thousands of people. The parade was followed by an official luncheon at which Lord Gainford addressed the audience, telling them that if the Germans were to be beaten and victory achieved then as much money as possible had to be raised.

Unbeknownst to many in the town, two famous guests stayed in Darlington over the weekend which saw the launch of the War Weapons Week. The actor Frank Lawton and his actress wife Evelyn Laye spent the weekend together in Darlington. At the outbreak of war Lawton had joined the Army as a private, but had recently been commissioned and was on special duties in the Darlington district at the time. His wife was the chair of the naval section of ENSA and gave dedicated service to the Royal Navy and the Royal Marines during the war. Her husband continued with his military duties, but also found the time to star in the highly creditable propaganda movie *Went the Day Well?* in 1942.

The War Weapons Week got off to a fantastic start with almost £300,000 promised towards the £650,000 total. Banks and other local companies had been responsible for some £242,000 of this sum (eight of these subscriptions had consisted of £25,000 each). Other promises made up the remaining sum.

The people of Darlington threw their efforts firmly behind the fundraising efforts which took place to aid the nation's war effort. The amount of money raised across north-east England through voluntary contributions was nothing short of remarkable. By the middle of June 1941, for example, the people of Darlington had contributed £2,218,957 to the War Savings Fund. This amounted to a contribution of £28 8s 11d per head of population in the town. In the week leading up to 20 June the people of Darlington had contributed the sum of £25,628 to the fund.

The headmaster of Darlington Grammar School had other concerns on his mind. He stated that the wartime situation was having a noted impact on the boys of the school, especially the older ones. Dr Hare claimed that with the future becoming more uncertain the older boys

Frank Lawton and his wife Evelyn Laye at home in 1942. (The Tatler)

had suffered from something of a lack of confidence and the recent abandonment of the Civil Service exams had exacerbated this. Dr Hare also believed that the air raid warnings were having a serious effect upon the older boys who were preparing to sit examinations and that this could mar their future careers and lives.

Lawton and his wife in their Dig for Victory cabbage patch. (The Tatler)

*The Lawton's
and their
chickens.*
(The Tatler)

There were shortages of food and many other essential items during wartime, and one that caused some concern and consternation in Darlington was the news that from 11 January 1941 the town's butchers were to close for the sale of meat on Tuesdays. The closure was to be in place until further notice. The decision was taken by the Butchers' Association in consultation with the Food Committee. The announcement was concerning not only because of the additional hardship, but also because it seemed to imply that supplies were insufficient.

With food rationing being tightened it became even more necessary for many people to grow their own foods and become more self-sufficient. While people were encouraged to Dig for Victory they were also encouraged where possible to raise their own livestock. Pig clubs and hen-rearing proved hugely popular throughout the war and it was no different in Darlington and Teesdale. The government, however, was keen to regularise dealings and at the end of January a number of accredited poultry breeding stations were named. These breeders sold only hatching eggs, day-old chicks and birds which were from blood-tested stock with a record of guaranteed egg production. The Darlington area seems to have been particularly well provided for as there were two stations in the village of Haughton-le-Skerne. They were Mr J.R. Banks of Willow Poultry Farm, 9 The Green, and Mr W. Dixon of Sandgarth Poultry Farm.

The food situation continued to attract attention and much comment. With the dramatic increase in the loss of ships at sea, the conservation, preservation and wise use of food supplies was of key concern to many local authorities. Darlington, however, voted against the use of communal feeding centres in February. Councillor Lyonnette sought to have the matter referred back to committee but was soundly defeated. Plans were in place for emergency feeding, but Councillor Lyonnette argued that it was a mistake to assume that communal feeding would result in some people getting more than their fair share because the bulk of the food used would be unrationed. Alderman T.E.B. Bates, however, argued that they had not adopted communal feeding as there was no provision for the handing over of coupons when a meal was obtained away from home. Somewhat missing the point, Alderman Bates continued by saying that the public assistance scheme had already spent between £8,000-£12,000 on establishing an emergency scheme which would, in the event of an emergency, see seven centres opened and manned in order to provide food and sleeping accommodation for 2,500 people. He added, without supplying any evidence, that this number could easily be doubled. Councillor Best supported Lyonnette's proposal, arguing that what was already being done to feed schoolchildren could be rolled out for adults with three centres at first until people got used to it.

The decision not to have communal feeding centres was strongly opposed by the general committee of Darlington's Labour Party. On 24 February 1941 the committee wrote to the council strongly urging them to reconsider the matter. The committee also complained about the inequalities in the meat rationing system which resulted in restaurants being able to obtain far more when compared to the meagre supply available to household consumers. This clearly eroded the 'fair shares for all' message of rationing because it was only the fairly well-off who could afford to eat out.

Most shopkeepers coped reasonably well with the rationing system and the new regulations which governed their hours of business and other matters. Others, however, did not and seemed determined to flout the rules. On 6 March, Robert Thornberry of Whinfield Road, Haughton-le-Skerne, was fined the sum of 10s with 12s 6d costs for the crime of failing to close his shop on a Sunday. When Mr Thornberry was caught out by the inspector, he was at home ill and had left the shop in the charge of a Miss Wilson. When accused of the offence, Miss Wilson told the inspector: 'We are fed up with the trouble with the ration books and one thing and another. We will lock up the damned shop and live on fresh air.'[10]

Concerns over rationing were only one frustration which was in evidence in the Darlington area in 1941. Some in authority were becoming increasingly concerned over what they perceived as a decline in moral standards.

With increasing numbers of Darlington men in the forces there was concern among the members of the corporation that wives of soldiers were using their husband's service as an excuse to neglect paying their rates on time, or at all. On 12 March the Town Clerk, Mr H. Hopkins, appeared at Darlington magistrates applying for distress orders against a number of cases of non-payment of rates for families where the breadwinner was in the forces. The Clerk argued that in many cases wives had the idea that they could neglect to pay their rates and defend their behaviour because their husband was serving. The debts in question now ranged from £3 to over £11. Continuing, Mr Hopkins stated that although he hated to say it, many of these women were better off financially now their husbands were serving than they had been previously; despite the increased costs of living, women now had extra income in the form of an allowance, in addition to the increased wages which were now being paid, while having no husband at home to keep. He also emphasised that the War Office had already made special provisions for those who were suffering hardship. The bench subsequently granted Mr Hopkins' application, with the Town Clerk assuring the magistrates that corporation officials would not be overly harsh in enforcing the orders and would accept outstanding sums in reasonable payments.

On 28 July 1941, a large exercise was carried out by the Darlington Home Guard, one of many such exercises. This particular exercise began at 3am when reports came through that enemy paratroops had landed at an airfield and captured the administrative block, although they had failed to capture the runways or the rest of the airfield. A Home Guard company immediately counter-attacked and successfully overcame the occupying force after a fierce struggle. At 8am an observation post reported a further landing on the other side of the town where the paratroops intended to capture a park so that further forces could be landed. The remainder of the battalion were ordered to repel this new threat. According to the umpires, the Home Guard fought well and there were many exciting encounters; the exercise revealed that the Home Guard had made great strides since its formation just over a year ago. The final verdict was that if enemy paratroops landed in the district the Darlington Home Guard would give a good account of itself. The exercise was said to have been of a realistic nature with a determined attempt by enemy paratroops to capture several key locations.

With travel restrictions and petrol rationing, the public transport system in Darlington had suffered tremendous strain and, as a result, there had been complaints to Darlington Rural District Council over congestion at the Leadyard bus station. The council took the decision to look into the matter and although it expressed the hope that a solution could be found, it did not seem to be overly hopeful. The same meeting also heard that, because of the increased wartime demand for bus services, the previous restrictions placed upon the ABC bus services on the Darlington-Chilton route were to be removed, meaning the ABC buses would be able to pick-up and drop-off passengers on an equal footing with the rival United services.

The problems afflicting public transport in Darlington continued into September 1941 when great difficulty was experienced in maintaining the town's trolley-bus services due to a shortage of staff. Despite this, there was strong resistance from Darlington Corporation's Transport Department to the training of women to act as drivers. Despite the fact that women were increasingly being accepted into a large number of jobs from which they had hitherto been barred, the manager stated that he did 'not expect that any immediate steps will be taken to train women as drivers'. He justified this decision, stating that he had 'not heard of any women being trained elsewhere as drivers of trolley-buses'.[11] He did seek to defend the Corporation by claiming that women were employed as conductresses on the majority of the trolley-buses in the town.

With Britain facing possible defeat in the war, there was a marked distaste among many of the population for those perceived to be shirking their duty to King and country. The conscientious objectors tribunals, however, tended to look on genuine cases with some understanding, though this was in itself sometimes tainted by that same distaste. On 6 November 1941 the tribunal at Newcastle heard the case of a Darlington insurance clerk, J.W. Jackson of 11 Clarendon Road. Mr Jackson expressed a desire for work on the land, but preferably with other pacifists. Judge Richardson told him that he would receive a very narrow viewpoint if he only associated with pacifists. Replying to this, Mr Jackson answered that he was prepared to work with non-pacifists but stubbornly added that he preferred the company of pacifists. Judge Richardson judged his case genuine and recommended he be conditionally registered for land work.

Although national politics was largely suspended during the course of the war, this was not the case in all local politics and throughout the war the steady process of local government which saw different councillors elected as mayor continued. In early November 1941, for example, the Town Council elected the new Mayor of Darlington, Councillor Barnett Jackson. The councillor had been in business in Darlington for twenty-two years and had been a member of the council since 1930. The decision to elect Councillor Jackson was unanimous, despite the somewhat incongruous fact that he actually lived in Gosforth, Newcastle.

With more work available to local engineering firms and longer hours being worked, pay had increased dramatically and there were concerns that some of the workers, especially the younger ones, were spending this extra on alcohol with a subsequent decrease in morals and behaviour. In mid-February 1942, the mutilated body of Cathleen Page Harburn (24) was found on the railway line at Piercebridge Station. Cathleen, known as Kitty, was a single woman who worked at Robert Stephenson and Hawthorns Ltd. On the night in question, Saturday 6 February, she had gone to a dance at Piercebridge along with colleagues, two female and one male. The four young people had each consumed three half-pints of beer, two small ports and a small rum and peppermint.

The man, John Hunt (24), who worked as a turner, told the subsequent inquest that neither he nor his companions were inebriated, but they were 'happy' when they left the dance. He explained how they had to cross the line to catch the Darlington train and that, hearing a train approaching, he had run across. He turned to find that two of the girls, Teresa Downs (19) and Winifred Williamson (22), had joined him, but there was no sign of Kitty. A goods train passed through shortly after he had crossed the line. Although they searched for Kitty, they were unable to find her and so boarded the Darlington train when it arrived. Mr Hunt said the thought that she had been struck by the train had not occurred to them. The jury returned a verdict of accidental death but was scathing in its criticism of the group, saying that they were not in their sober senses and had consumed too much alcohol. Following the jury's verdict, the coroner berated Mr Hunt, telling him he hoped it would serve as a lesson which he would never forget. He also called the two young women before him and was addressing their conduct when Ms Williamson interrupted him asking if she might object. She was brusquely told that she could object as much as she liked but the views expressed were those of the jury.

Although preoccupation with the war dominated in Darlington, there were other events which served to give cheer to some of the population. On 23 December 1942, for example, Mr and Mrs Shinn of Woodland Road celebrated a very special landmark birthday when Mrs Shinn's mother turned 100. It was a year of celebration for the family as Mr Shinn's own mother had herself turned 100 in September. Both women had been born in London and both had given birth to seven children. Both women had lived in London throughout the blitz, with Mrs Shinn's mother being bombed out of her home. Mr and Mrs Shinn had lived in Darlington since 1914 with Mr Shinn having been employed as the Northern Divisional Inspector of the Ministry of Health Insurance Department. Mr Shinn retired in 1931 and in the same year he was awarded the Companionship of the Imperial Service Order.

With the fascination that many in the town had for the RAF it is no surprise that fundraising for the force was always popular. Darlington's Wings for Victory campaign began on Saturday, 29 May 1943 and the Mayor, Councillor B. Jackson, was pleased to be able to announce at the opening ceremony that nearly half of the £600,000 target figure had already been raised. The Mayor announced that some £283,000 had been promised and a further £100,000 investment had been recommended by the Darlington Corporation Finance Committee. Other major investments had included £25,000 apiece from Barclays, Lloyds, Midland, Martins, National Provincial and Westminster banks. The opening ceremony included a large parade by the men and women of the armed and civilian forces and so great was the enthusiasm that the parade itself stretched for three miles. Taking the salute was Air Vice-Marshal G.E. Brookes, RCAF, the commanding officer of 6 (RCAF) Group. Among the speakers at the ceremony was Darlington MP, Mr C.U. Peat, who paid wholesome tribute to the men of the RAF.

Overseeing the system of rationing continued to be a time-consuming and taxing effort, with ration books having to be reissued on a yearly basis, the work faced by local authorities was huge although they seemed to have managed fairly well. At the end of May 1943, the Darlington food officials were not contemplating any changes in the system, and the Food Executive Officer, Mr T.H. Laverick, told the local press that the reissue was going smoothly. By midday on Thursday, 27 May, the local authorities had issued 12,000 of the 20,000 new ration books that were scheduled for issue in that week. Queues at the office were not long and the majority of applicants were seen very quickly, with the longest wait being an hour.

By 4 June, the tally in the Wings for Victory campaign stood at £632,000, and it was hoped in some quarters that the town might even be able to reach the £1,000,000 mark. By the end of the campaign on 11 June, the final tally was £888,209; not quite the figure of £1,000,000 that the Mayor had hoped for, but still a very creditable amount that meant an average of £11 6s 6d per head of population had been donated. One of the final cheques to be handed over was for £300 16*s* 3*d*, which had been raised by the local Licensed Victuallers' Association. The Mayor declared himself both happy and proud of the people of Darlington and their magnificent effort.

Sunday, 26 September was to be commemorated as 'Battle of Britain Sunday' and in Darlington there was a parade scheduled to give thanks to the RAF for their actions in 1940. The parade was to be followed by a service at the parish church. Due to the size of the parade it was not possible to admit members of the public to the church and so the service was broadcast via loudspeakers into Market Place. Following the service the salute was to be taken by Group Captain G.D. Ross, RCAF, on High Row.

October 1943 opened with yet another tragedy on the roads. An inquest heard that Richard Coggins (63), a retired schoolmaster of School House, Newbiggin-in-Teesdale and a member of Barnard Castle Rural Council, was knocked down by a car as he ran across the road to catch a bus. Councillor Coggins had been in a garage when he heard his bus approaching and ran out into the path of the car; the driver was held blameless.

Despite the fact that 1943 was the year when it finally looked like the tide of war was changing in favour of the Allies, there were still severe shortages in some areas. In Darlington at the end of November and beginning of December there had been concerns expressed over the fact that there were little or no facilities for the provision of teas and light refreshments between the hours of 6-10pm. Representatives of the town's cafes and hotels met with the town council to discuss this need but unanimously agreed that, owing to the difficulties of staffing and securing of adequate supplies, it was impossible for the catering establishments to remain open and provide these services. It was agreed that enquiries would be made to see if a hall or some other building might be bought or rented by the corporation in order to provide these facilities along with music and similar entertainment. A letter had been received from the Ministry of Food stating that it would be acceptable for the town's British Restaurant to be opened in the evenings to provide light refreshments as long as the costs were covered locally.

As we have seen, crime continued to be a problem during wartime but although there were exceptions, the majority of Darlington folk conducted themselves in a far more encouraging manner and ensured that they made a positive contribution to the war effort. At the end of March 1944 the boys and girls of Egglestone village school and some of the members of Middleton-in-Teesdale young farmers' club featured in a film produced by the Ministry of Information. The film debuted in London on 24 March at a display which was opened by the Duke of Norfolk. The film was made at the behest of the Ministry of Agriculture and was to be shown across the country in war factories, cinemas and town halls.

One of the yearly government-encouraged campaigns, the Salute the Soldier campaign, lasted for a week and was intended to raise funds for the Army. These weekly campaigns (Weapons for War, Salute the Soldier, Warship Week, Wings for Victory, etc) relied on a mixture of generosity and public spirit which was further encouraged by a keen sense of competition between the various communities which took part. The Salute the Soldier campaign was boosted on Saturday, 13 May 1944 by a display of tanks, armoured cars, guns and other vehicles which was held on the Bridge Street clearance site. The Darlington Home Guard band played at the event and there was a very good turnout. By the end of 15 May the target of £750,000 had been smashed with £818,595 having been reached by the end of Saturday and the hope that £900,000 would eventually be reached when the final tally was made. This would beat Stockton's figure per head of population and would place Darlington in the lead in the competition for the county banner. The campaign received particular prominence as it was obvious to most that the second front was only weeks or months away and that the army would be requiring ever-more ammunition, weapons and equipment.

Shortly after D-Day the Germans began launching V1 flying bombs against southern England. Although these weapons were inaccurate they were a worrying development as, at first, defences struggled to come to terms with them and there were early casualties. On 28 July 1944 Darlington received its first batch of people who had been evacuated from London due to the V-weapon attacks on the capital and southern England. The first party consisted of 689 mothers and children and by the start of September there were some 6,250 evacuees from the London area in the town. By and large, this new wave of evacuees received a warm and understanding welcome from both the authorities and the people of the town, despite the additional strain which it placed upon the local authorities.

With wounded men returning home from the fighting in Normandy, the local charities in Darlington quickly set about intensifying their fundraising efforts for organisations such as the Red Cross. Others took a more proactive stance, directly interacting with the wounded. Since its inception in 1943 the Darlington 20 Club had made a great contribution to the town's war effort and did a great deal of fundraising during the war. In September 1944, the club played host to twenty wounded soldiers from various northern hospitals. The servicemen were entertained to lunch at the Imperial Hotel on the occasion of the club's first anniversary. Guests of honour at the dinner included the Mayor, Councillor A. Trees, Major A.B. Leake, Darlington Battalion, the Home Guard, and Mr Fred Reed, the president of the rotary club.

The start of December 1944 saw the opening of the new luxury NAAFI (Navy, Army and Air Force Institute) Club in Park Street which had cost £10,000 to construct and furnish and replaced the Nissen huts which had hitherto been used. The club was formally opened by Darlington's MP, Mr C.U. Peat. After the opening, a reception took place hosted by the Mayor (Councillor James Blumer) and Air Chief Marshal Sir R. Brooke-Popham, the president of the council of NAAFI. Mr Peat paid extensive tribute to the work of the voluntary organisations in helping the men and women in the services who were stationed around Darlington. He went on to say that the club was a magnificent addition and added that although some people claimed the club should have been built sooner, he wished to point out all the fundraising that had gone on for a variety of causes in the town meant that they had to really stretch themselves to fund the club. Lieutenant General Sir Edwin Morris, General Officer Commander-in-Chief of Northern Command added that one of the greatest successes in the war was the cooperation of civilian and services. Speaking on behalf of the Admiralty, Rear Admiral Sir Wellwood Maxwell added that the clubs set up in ports for the use of merchant seamen had been a great success, but that all sailors deserved the very best, no matter what their branch of service.

Late in 1944 there were concerns about the administration of the health department in Darlington. The complaints specifically targeted the Medical Officer of Health, Dr G.A. Dawson. They alleged that he lacked tact, was overly harsh in his treatment of subordinates and was unable to work well with others. As a result, the council had appointed a special sub-committee to inquire into the matter and in early December the doctor appeared before them. The matter seems to have been complicated and the committee, yet to reach a conclusion, had adjourned until the following week in order to give Dr Dawson the opportunity to present his case in a fuller manner. However, Dr Dawson was found gassed in his garage before he could re-appear. Giving evidence at the subsequent inquest, Dr Dawson's solicitor, Mr A.C. Hinks, stated that he was preparing his client's answer to the allegation, adding that he did have a full answer, and that he was confident that Dr Dawson would be cleared of the allegations. Dr Dawson was aged 46 and had been Medical Officer at Darlington for eighteen years. The inquest heard how Dr Dawson had been worried about the inquiry and had been suffering from insomnia. The coroner returned a verdict that Dr Dawson had committed suicide while the balance of his mind was disturbed and added that the matter which was concerning him 'was not worth the loss of a single night's sleep'.[12]

With aircraft from nearby airfields constantly having to be tested before and after operations over Germany it was inevitable that accidents which affected those on the ground would occur. On the evening of 13 January 1945, Pilot Officer William Stuart McMullen, RCAF, took off with his crew on a cross-country training flight. As the Lancaster X (KB793, NA-E) of 428 (RCAF) Squadron approached RAF Middleton St George, the port inner engine caught fire and McMullen gave the order to abandon the aircraft. At the time the bomber was at 2,500ft over Acklam. By the time the final crewman, Flight Sergeant Llewelyn, the flight engineer, was ready to bale out, the aircraft was down to just 600ft. The flight engineer looked over at his skipper and gestured at him to join him in leaving the aircraft. McMullen, however, was fearful that the bomber might crash on Darlington and elected to remain with the aircraft. According to later reports from the Air Ministry he shouted to his comrade that 'It's only me for it. There are thousands down below.' By the time he had cleared the town he was too low to bale out and he was killed when the Lancaster crashed at Lingfield Farm at 8.49pm. An eye-witness in the town stated that the bomber seemed to circle briefly and appeared to be likely to come down in the town, but it turned east and crashed a few seconds afterwards. Pilot Officer McMullen was a 33-year-old married man with a young daughter and was from Lulu Island, British Columbia (although reportedly born in Toronto). His body was discovered, still in his pilot's seat, some 120 yards from the wreckage but his flying boots were discovered still attached to the rudder pedals. The official report noted that the pilot had retained sufficient control to avoid the built-up area of Darlington.

The people of Darlington were quickly convinced that this gallant Canadian plot had willingly sacrificed his own life in order to save their own and the local newspapers featured letters from townspeople urging some form of memorialisation for the gallant airman. The town, led by the Mayor, Councillor James Blumer, rallied round the cause and speedily raised funds, under the auspices of the 20 Club, and demanded that the brave action of Pilot Officer McMullen be recognised and that the town's appreciation be shown in a tangible form, either as a memorial to the pilot, or in the form of assistance to his family back in Canada. Demonstrating the strength of feeling in Darlington, the Gallant Airman Fund was set up and quickly raised the sum of £1,000 which was to be sent to McMullen's widow and daughter. McMullen's widow, Thelma, refused the gift, however, stating that she would feel better if it were put to use in providing aid to war-ravaged Britain.[13] Blumer later wrote to Thelma McMullen praising her husband's actions, concluding that his splendid courage in sacrificing his own life for the people of Darlington would never be forgotten in the town.[14]

The 20 Club had launched the fundraising with a cheque for £100 and had advertised the fund around the town. One of the more unusual methods of fundraising was thought up by a Darlington hotel landlord who began charging 6d per look at his young two-legged pig. In just a week he had raised £18 for the fund.

As 8 May 1945 dawned, the people of Darlington became aware that today was indeed Victory in Europe Day (VE-Day, although most of the press described it as V-Day at the time) and housewives made hurried preparations to organise street and house parties. Some men turned up at work for early shifts but were turned away, although at first the atmosphere was muted. Heavy rain did not help but this cleared by 3pm. Despite this, many people were on the streets from an early hour, mainly gathering supplies. Every street in the town centre was bedecked with flags and bunting and almost every house was decorated with the Union flag. Churchill's speech seems to have been the catalyst for people to

Pilot Officer William Stuart McMullen, RCAF (Northern Echo)

begin the celebrations and across the town people spilled out into impromptu street parties with dancing and eating.

As the day wore on the celebrations became more raucous and Darlington appears to have been the most celebratory community in Co. Durham. Thousands gathered in Market Place for a dance and another large crowd assembled at High Row. Poles and lampposts were climbed, flags flown, songs sung, musical instruments brought out into the streets and two Belisha beacons were used in a football/rugby match which was described as 'extremely rough'. In Market Square the council had arranged a stage with a public address system to control the dance, but the stage was invaded and taken over by men from the Welsh Guards who sang with great gusto. The celebrations grew somewhat rowdy and fireworks were let off among the crowd outside the Central Hall, causing some revellers to take shelter by climbing to the top of air raid shelters. The rowdiness resulted in injuries and Darlington Memorial Hospital was filled with an influx of casualties ranging from people who had been struck by thrown bottles, to those who had collided with other revellers.

Several landmarks, including the clock tower of the Town Hall and St Cuthbert's Church, were floodlit with two searchlights outside the Town Hall forming a V – for victory – in the sky, and the spectacle, unseen in blacked-out wartime Britain, attracted large crowds. The crowds around these locations entertained themselves by holding communal singalongs and the crowds did not disperse, despite more rain, until after midnight when a thunderstorm raged overhead.

Although people were keen to celebrate, there was something of an ambivalence for many. So many Darlington men had lost their lives and many families were in mourning despite the celebrations. The day also brought tragedy when an army lorry overturned at Winston on its way into Darlington. Three soldiers were injured and an ATS officer, 26-year-old W/O2 Doris Newell-Smith was killed.

Others wished to express their thankfulness on a more sober manner and at one point some 1,200 people gathered at St Cuthbert's Church for a thanksgiving service. The second day of the national holiday was quieter and, once again, affected by the weather. With rationing, supplies were still hard to come by but there were still a number of street and house parties and the inevitable dances were quickly organised and held along with a great deal of community singing. The highlights of the second day of celebrations included another dance in Market Place, accompanied by both a military band and by records played over loudspeaker while in South Park the rink was illuminated for a roller-skating dance.

Darlington had made a substantial contribution to the war through its engineering and steel plants and through the actions of the many men and women who had joined the forces. Outside the town, the local farmers had made a contribution through their effort to follow the government's advice to produce the food vital to keeping Britain in the war. The town had not suffered anywhere near the level of bombing which other communities in Northeast England had experienced.

Brunswick Street VE-Day party. (Northern Echo)

Right: *Pouring jelly which refused to set at the Brunswick Street VE-Day party.* (Northern Echo)

Below: *Brunswick Street VE-Day party.* (Northern Echo)

Scene at the Brunswick-street (Darlington) VE-Day tea party. Pouring out the jelly which refused to set.

Children at the Victory party in Slater's Buildings, Bondgate, Darlington.—[N.D.]

Slater's Buildings VE-Day street party. (Northern Echo)

The victory party in Hundens-lane East, Darlington.—[N.D.]

Victory party in Hunden's Lane. (Northern Echo)

The Regional Commissioner for the North, in his official report at the end of the war, stated that Darlington had no civilians killed in raids, only two people injured badly enough to be detained in hospital and eight people slightly injured.

The General Election held on 5 July 1945 brought about a resounding victory for the Labour Party with Clement Atlee replacing Winston Churchill as Prime Minister. In Darlington the sitting Conservative MP, Charles Peat, MC, lost his seat to Labour's David Hardman.[15] Peat had held Darlington since 1931 and was a popular figure, a well-known cricketer. He had served as Principal Private Secretary to Winston Churchill and had spearheaded the wartime campaign to salvage 100 million books for the war effort. Britain's new Prime Minister, Clement Atlee, announced at midnight on 14/15 August that Japan had surrendered and that the war was finally over. Once again, there were two days of public holiday and once again, people rushed out onto the streets, but the celebrations across Darlington and other areas were more muted than those that had taken place for VE-Day. Possibly some people saw the greater threat being Nazi Germany and viewed the war with Japan as one which was far away from Britain, but for the many residents who still had loved ones in action in the Far East the news came as a blessed relief. The main reason for the more muted celebrations, however, was the lack of supplies, especially beer. Many pubs in Darlington and Barnard Castle had signs outside proclaiming that they had no beer due to wartime shortages.

Despite the lack of beer, most communities in the area still arranged some sort of party with dancing, finger food and music. Bonfires and fireworks were a feature of the celebrations as night descended. In Darlington, the *Northern Despatch* claimed that the first instinct of many women in the town upon hearing the news was to grab their shopping bags and head out early to secure food supplies. Thus, a large proportion of those lining the streets during the early part of the day were in fact queuing for food and there were large queues outside the bakers, butchers, fishmongers and grocers shops. The newspaper

VJ-Day cartoon. (Northern Despatch)

Members of South Durham Boys' Brigade at camp in Croft on VJ-Day.
(Northern Despatch)

reported that so important was the need to lay in supplies that even men were seen in the shopping queues! Some of the men obviously found it thirsty work and those pubs which did have beer supplies soon had queues outside them too. The shopping scenes in Darlington were common across the whole area. There were many shortages; bread and tobacco were in particularly short supply and greengrocers found that they were besieged. In the evening, many people travelled into Darlington from neighbouring villages.

The *Darlington and Stockton Times* reported that it was a curious day in Barnard Castle with flags and bunting flying, military bands playing, a loudspeaker van touring the streets and an ice-cream stall set up in Market Place, but the shortage of beer in nearly every licensed premises put a slight dampener on the occasion. Some of the pubs opened for an hour, but many residents could be seen on the streets with frustrated expressions. In Darlington, the day closure of many public houses resulted in a more mellow atmosphere than VE-Day when overly boisterous crowds had caused £200 of damage in Market Place. On this occasion the celebrations were good humoured and continued until after midnight.

In Market Place it was so crowded that it was difficult for dancers to express themselves, but from 7pm the crowd enjoyed the music from the band of the 10ʰ Hussars which had recently returned from Germany. An hour later, hooters and sirens throughout the town sounded the all-clear and church bells rang. The derelict area where the slums of Bridge Street had been cleared played host to an estimated 8,000 people who gathered around a huge bonfire which was lit by the Mayor at 9pm. The bonfire went on for three hours, with rockets and Verey lights being fired off from a house on the south side of Bridge Street.

Building a VJ-Day Bonfire at Cockerton.—[N.D.]

Bonfire being built at Cockerton.
(Northern Despatch)

Unloading rubbish and wood in Park-street, Darlington, for a VJ-Day bonfire.—[D.N.]

Collecting bonfire materials on Park Street on VJ-Day.
(Northern Despatch)

Dancing in Darlington Market Place on VJ-Day. (Northern Despatch)

The newspaper reported that another possible reason for the more subdued celebrations was that people were aware of the difficulties left facing Britain despite the victory, the increased shortages since VE-Day were a sure sign of that. A cartoon in the *Northern Despatch* conveyed these concerns vividly.

Cartoon on VJ-Day. (Northern Despatch)

CHAPTER 3

Evacuees and Bombing Raids

One of the earliest examples of the war affecting ordinary life was the evacuation of children and vulnerable people from many urban areas which were adjudged to be vulnerable to aerial attack. All along the east coast of England evacuations started the weekend that the war began.

Although Darlington, somewhat mystifyingly given its industrial character and geographical position close to the coast, had not been included in the first wave of evacuation, local schoolchildren still had their education disrupted. Schools were closed across the town so that air raid shelters could be constructed in their grounds. By the end of October 1939 nearly every school had a shelter and the children could begin to return to school. Many of the teachers had assisted the ARP services in constructing and organising the shelters and their efforts had saved the town a great deal of money with their efforts.

There were still problems, however, with teacher shortages and some schools having been taken over for ARP and civil defence duties. As a result of this it was decided that 10 and 11 year olds would attend full-time, but those younger pupils would attend on a half-time basis. The youngest, those under 7 years of age, were free to attend on a half-time basis, or not to attend at the decision of their parents. The disruption to their schooling continued throughout much of the war and caused many problems, largely with minor crimes being committed by bored youngsters who were not only not at school but were also suffering from a lack of parental guidance due to the war.

Not only was Darlington not included in the initial evacuation scheme but the countryside of Teesdale found itself playing host to evacuees from other areas. A number of the better-cared for evacuees who had found themselves in the area enjoyed days out from time to time with many enjoying the experiences of the countryside. In early September 1940 several evacuees from the Sunderland area who were staying near Richmond were brought on an excursion to Piercebridge. The youths enjoyed the experience and were said to be both happy and healthy in their new homes.

The Darlington area experienced its first air raid on the night of 26/27 August 1940 when eight High Explosive (HE) bombs were dropped in the vicinity of Haughton-le-Skerne and Sadberge. Two more HE bombs fell on the southern side of the Darlington-Stockton road at Great Burdon and three Incendiary Bombs (IB) fell into an oat field on the east side of Sadberge-Fighting Cocks road. There was little damage from the bombs, but one which fell between Haughton-le-Skerne and Sadberge had a delayed fuse and exploded at 6.35am, killing several heifers and horses.

At 1.00am on 5 September, bombs, mainly IB, fell on Darlington. Several small fires were started in residential properties and at a number of industrial sites. The fires were quickly brought under control and there was little damage. At Darlington Rolling Mills an employee received burns from an IB. Several farms on the outskirts of the town were also hit by IBs and a haystack and some wooden outbuildings were destroyed because the fire brigade could not access a supply of water. In Memory Lane there were four craters left by HE bombs, but no injuries were reported.

On 15 September 1940, with the Battle of Britain raging, the people of the area witnessed RAF fighters attacking Luftwaffe aircraft that were attempting to raid several sites in the Northeast. At 1.36pm an Me110D was shot down and crashed at Streatlam near Barnard Castle; the explosion when the aircraft crashed injured a workman. The two crew were captured and taken to Barnard Castle Police Station. Many of the aircraft ejected their bombs when they came under attack and there were a number of civilian casualties scattered across the Northeast, including William Armstrong Harrison, a 9-year-old evacuee from

Hebburn who was killed by shrapnel at Toft Hill, Etherley, near Barnard Castle.

Many Darlington families did evacuate their children to safer areas, some as part of the later official evacuations, while others sent their children away privately, sometimes accompanying them, renting rural properties. For most families who had children evacuated, the distance separating them was large but not insurmountable; for one Darlington mother, however, the only way to reach her 15-year-old daughter was by the BBC radio service. Mrs Eckford of Clifton Road visited the BBC studios in Newcastle to record a radio message for her daughter, Sheila, who was in Canada. Sheila had been among hundreds of children who were evacuated to Canada at the start of the war and was staying with a teacher in Hamilton, Ontario. Mrs Eckford had received several letters from her daughter in which she had expressed her happiness in Canada and related how she was doing well at school, particularly in French.

At 6.40pm on the evening of 5/6 January 1941, several HE and IBs were dropped on Darlington. Several small fires were started at the Faverdale Works of the LNER and at a bakehouse in Commerical Street. These fires, however, were quickly brought under control. Two HEs also fell onto the Faverdale Works but although one hit the gable end of a building, the damage was sparse – excepting several craters. Production at the Faverdale Works was disrupted by the presence of an unexploded bomb. The Stooperdale Works of the LNER, however, were badly damaged when an HE bomb fell on the boiler house.

While other parts of the Northeast suffered very badly, especially during the spring months of 1941, the Luftwaffe rarely targeted Darlington and few bombs fell on the town. This is not to say that the people were not disrupted by the nearby raids. The alarm frequently sounded and forced people to take shelter, resulting in stress and disrupted sleep. In the early hours of 14 March for example, a German bomber dropped eleven IBs on Darlington, but the resultant fires were quickly brought under control and there was no damage or casualties.

In the early hours of 12 May 1941 Darlington once again had a small number of bombs dropped upon it. It is known that two HEs fell on Beaumont Hill near to the LNER line but, once again, no damage was done. Compared to many other Northeast communities, Darlington had escaped very lightly in the spring of 1941. The failure to attack the Darlington area was somewhat mystifying as the area was home to a number of important industrial concerns which were working on important war work.

In the early hours of 1 May 1942 the people of Darlington once again heard the air raid sirens wailing. A small force of enemy bombers roamed about over Northeast England, seemingly dropping bombs at random in what was a widely scattered raid. Once again, Darlington escaped fairly lightly with just four HEs dropped at the junction of Blackwell Lane and Blackwell Village Road. Damage was caused to several residential properties and two people suffered minor injuries.

Up to September 1942, only two people had suffered minor injuries as a result of bombing in Darlington that year, but on the night of 19 September there was another raid over the Northeast. The anti-aircraft defences around the town went into action, but two exploding anti-aircraft shells exploded in the town and three people were injured by shell splinters.

On the night of 11/12 March 1943 the Luftwaffe returned to the Northeast and the people of Darlington who left their shelters witnessed the sight of a German bomber being shot down over the town. A Dornier Do217E was held by searchlights and a Beaufighter night fighter of 219 Squadron engaged the German bomber and shot it down. The bomber crashed at High Grange Farm, Great Stainton, at 11.25pm. The crew of four all baled out and were quickly captured. Two were injured and were sent under guard to the Military Hospital at Winterton while the other two were detained at Stockton Police Station.[1]

With the V-Weapon offensive seeing missiles hitting the south-east of England and causing heavy casualties, the decision was taken to evacuate thousands of children and the vulnerable from the capital.

The vast majority of these new evacuees found themselves sent to the Northeast. The attacks lasted throughout the spring and early summer of 1944. This new wave of evacuees found welcoming homes in Darlington and Teesdale and many reported how happy they were at what they experienced whilst staying in the area.

October 1944 also saw large numbers of the London folk who had been evacuated to the North following the V-weapon attacks return home, but by the end of the month approximately 3,800 still remained in the town. Of the 689 who had arrived in the first wave of evacuees, the majority, some 600, had returned home. The majority of the evacuees expressed their thanks for the warm and understanding welcome that they had experienced from the people of Darlington.

By early 1945 people had relaxed their attitude towards the possibility of air raids, but in the early hours of Sunday 4 March, seventy German night fighters roamed over eastern England for a period of over three hours. The defences were caught napping. Several residential houses in Darlington were damaged by cannon and machine-gun fire and a woman was injured.

Despite the very real fears that the people of Darlington had about being bombed, the area was very lightly treated by the Luftwaffe and the town did not suffer anywhere near the levels of bombing or casualties that were experienced in many other Northeast communities. By the end of the war there had been no fatalities in Darlington County Borough as a result of enemy bombing while casualties amounted to just two who were injured and required to be detained in hospital while eight others were slightly injured.

CHAPTER 4

Wartime Crime

Although the war changed many people's lives in Darlington instantly, many aspects of life continued as normal. Crime continued in evidence and the local police and judiciary maintained their regular duties. On 15 September, for example, Darlington Police Court heard a case of abandonment and neglect. Mr Thomas L. Swainston (29) had been charged with abandoning his wife and three children at their home at Backhouse Street. Mr Swainston had left his family with no means of financial support and the local authorities had therefore paid the sum of £11 16s 10d in relief for the upkeep of the family. Mr Swainston was found guilty of the charge and was sentenced to two months' hard labour.

There had been a spate of thefts of motor vehicles by soldiers and on 15 January 1940 Mr Robert Anderson, the presiding magistrate at Darlington, commented that steps would have to be taken to stop the trend. Mr Anderson had just heard the case of Signalman John Hardcastle, a 23-year-old soldier with the Royal Corps of Signals, who had been accused of attempting to take a motor vehicle without the owner's consent. Signalman Hardcastle had been seen by detectives, together with three comrades, to walk up to a car which belonged to a local butcher and which had been parked in Bondgate. The four soldiers got into the car, with Hardcastle in the driving seat. They were immediately arrested. Hardcastle claimed that he had merely intended to sound the horn to alert the owner so that they could ask for a lift back to their barracks. An Army officer from Hardcastle's unit testified that he had previously been of very good character, but he was found guilty and fined the sum of £2. The police had clearly mounted an operation targeting the area on the night in question because they had arrested another soldier on the same night for stealing a car from the same location. Alfred B. Low (33) of the Green Howards (Yorkshire Regiment) was remanded in custody until his case could be heard.

Despite the importance of food rationing there seems to have been a marked reluctance to be overly harsh with offenders during the first months in Darlington. At the start of February 1940 a Newcastle firm, Young's Confectionary Ltd, was charged with having illegally supplied sugar at their Darlington shop. The Town Clerk, Mr Hopkins, prosecuted and testified that on 16 January, 1lb of sugar had been supplied over the counter to a person who was not registered as a customer and no ration book or coupons were asked for by the clerk. Mr Hopkins was clearly eager for a harsh penalty as he reminded the bench that the possible punishment for such defendants, if found guilty, was six months' imprisonment or a fine of £100 before stating that, as this was a limited company, he could bring the directors before the bench to face imprisonment if found guilty. The magistrates, however, seem to have ignored the Town Clerk and fined the company £1.

Crime continued to exercise the local authorities and, on 29 February 1940, a sad case involving Darlington woman Jean Elizabeth Rogers (29), who was accused of bigamy, was heard at Leeds Assizes. Mrs Rogers had married a William Rogers at Darlington in 1932 but the marriage, from which there were two children, had been an unhappy one and the couple had agreed to separate in 1936. In 1939 Mrs Rogers was working as a barmaid in Harrogate and met a soldier, John Frederick Knightson (a man who apparently bore a marked resemblance to Gary Cooper) and the two went through a form of marriage at Knaresborough Register Office after a short acquaintance. After Knightson had been posted abroad, a photograph of the couple was published in the press because he apparently bore a resemblance to a film star; after suspicions were aroused and enquiries made, Mrs Rogers eventually admitted that she had been married before but said that she thought her and her husband were divorced. The prosecution established that she had made no enquiries about the supposed divorce. In a statement to the police, Mrs Rogers said that she had married Knightson because she had fallen in love with him and because he was going away. The Army allowance of 17s a week, she claimed, was not a factor and she had not even been aware of it before she and Knightson married. Finding her guilty and passing sentence, Mr Justice Cassels said that Rogers had deceived Knightson into thinking she was a single woman and that she had written her surname as if it was her maiden name. He concluded that: 'It was a gross and wicked deceit you practised upon that man, and I am bound to pass some kind of sentence on you.' Rogers was sentenced to prison for three months.[1]

Not only did the blackout lead to an increase in accidents, it also allowed those of a criminal persuasion additional scope in committing crimes. The presence of large numbers of conscripted men, often bored by service life, also added to the temptation to commit criminal acts. At the North Riding Quarters Sessions at Darlington on 4 April, the case of three soldiers of the Royal Corps of Signals accused theft and breaking and entering was heard. Such cases increased significantly as the blackout, combined with reduced policing, meant that criminals grew bolder. The accused, Ernest Evans (21), Thomas William Neal (26) and Aitkenhead (30) all pleaded guilty. Evans and Neal each pleaded guilty to five offences with another nineteen taken into consideration, while Aitkenhead pleaded guilty to three offences with another eight taken into consideration. Aitkenhead already had a criminal record, having been convicted of a crime in Canada and deported to England in 1933. The three men had worked together in several of the crimes and had stolen property and money to the value of £100. The men, it was said, had become involved because they found Army life boring and were looking for a change. One of the crimes involved damage to a telephone booth and its equipment; in the time of national emergency, this was a serious matter as it could have 'involved a breakdown in the civil defence'.[2] Neal, who had damaged the phone, was sentenced to three years penal servitude, Aitken to two years hard labour and Evans to three years in a borstal.

The concerns over the rise in crime which was blamed by some upon the growing numbers of servicemen in the Darlington area, continued throughout the first few months of 1940. The incidents of soldiers stealing motor vehicles which began in 1939 seems to have continued and become a somewhat persistent problem in Darlington. On the night of 19 April, a patrolling Darlington police constable saw a soldier having trouble restarting a car. He asked who the car belonged to and the soldier replied, 'Whose car do you think it is?' At this point three military policemen arrived on the scene and the soldier fled. He was apprehended and charged with having stolen the car, at which point he apologised. The soldier, Corporal Kenneth James Kerr Roy (25) appeared before magistrates on 22 April and Superintendent H. Huitson told the magistrates that information had recently come to light which made him ask for the accused to be remanded. It is unknown what this information was, but it could well have alluded to the corporal's possible criminal past. In 1938 a private in the King's Own Scottish Borderers named Kenneth James Kerr Roy had been charged with having stolen a suitcase and contents worth £7 7s 10d from the Victoria Barracks in Portsmouth before fleeing to Glasgow. It is impossible to say if this was the same man, but it seems likely.

Among the regulations which were put into place at this stage of the war, one of the most talked about was rationing. Although designed to ensure a fair share for all, there were problems inherent in the system. The rationing system placed butchers in a position of power over their customers since it was largely they who decided what was available and to whom. The process was meant to be fair but was widely open to manipulation and, for some members of the trade, greed got the better of them. The rationing system was overseen by local Food Control Committees which were made up of members of the local council, representatives from the butchery trade and representatives of the consumers. On 16 May 1940 a case of breaching the rationing orders was brought against two Darlington butchers. Even more serious was the fact that one of the accused occupied a seat on the committee.

Charles W. Jackson of Linden Avenue was the butchers' nominee on the committee and it was alleged that his brother, who was in charge of his Skinnergate shop at the time, sold chops to an inspector who was not a registered customer. In mitigation, it was argued that Charles Jackson was spending more than half of his time in public work. His solicitor admitted that there had been 'a technical breach of the regulations by him, but the prosecution resulted from something in the nature of a trap just before the shop closed on Saturday night'.[3] The defendant's brother, Robert, had served approximately 800 customers throughout the day and he thought that he had recognised the inspector as a customer. The defence of a technical breach was not an adequate one, but it seems that his public work did indeed provide some mitigation as Mr Jackson was fined the sum of £2 with a further £1 1s in costs.

A further case was heard on the same day when Mr Robert Sinclair of North Cowton was fined the far more substantial sum of £5 with £1 1s costs for selling chops to an inspector at his stall in Darlington covered market without asking him to produce a ration coupon.

Late May 1940 brought an interesting case before Darlington magistrates. The case concerned the very serious charge under the Defence Regulations. Because of the sensitive nature of the charges the case was heard in camera, with the magistrates clearing the court. Mr Henry J. Raymond (42) of 54 Danesmoor Crescent, Carmel Road, Darlington, a garrison engineer, both electrical and mechanical, faced two charges. The first was that of having in his possession a certain document, of which no details were given. The second involved communicating certain information that would, or could, be useful to the enemy. Once again the nature of the information was not disclosed due to security issues. All the magistrate would say was that the information and document were such that it was highly desirable that the proceedings against Mr Raymond be heard in camera and that no details of either the information or the document should be made public. Mr Raymond was subsequently found guilty on both charges. Surprisingly, given the nature of the charges against him, Mr Raymond was not given a custodial sentence but was fined £5 for the first offence, £25 for the second and ordered to pay costs of £4 6s 6d.

Despite the fact that the country was fighting for its continued existence and facing the greatest threat that it had ever faced, not everyone seems to have been concerned with the war and some were willing to continue their petty peacetime campaigns. In late October 1940 a Darlington solicitor, Mr Horace W. Wooler of Linden Avenue, appeared in court in a trial which concerned two incidents in which Mr Wooler had passed on information to the police about his neighbours. The police had duly cautioned a Mr Harold F. Wade, alleging that he had made a fire within 50ft of the highway, and a Mr Alexander Dunn, a van driver, alleging that he had left his engine running while making a delivery. In his testimony, Mr Wooler said that the van engine was 'making a terrific row'. Mr Wooler seems to have been a serial complainant and the defendant's solicitor asked him if it was not true that he was 'notorious in your district as a busybody, and is it your practice to make complaints of trivial matters about your neighbours?' Mr Wooler answered that he was not a busybody, adding that people in his street thought 'they can do as they like'. He did admit that he had made quite a lot of complaints, and when asked if there was a lot of noise in his neighbourhood he said, 'Yes, dogs, hooligans, aeroplanes.'[4] Quite clearly, Mr Wooler was indeed a busybody and one who, equally clearly, had a bee in his bonnet and was eager to make multiple complaints over trivial matters. The court dismissed the charges and the bench then awarded costs of a guinea against the police.

With the Battle of the Atlantic raging, and shipping being lost at an unsustainable rate, the need for strict enforcement of the food rationing system had never been more important. Many people found themselves before the magistrates bench facing charges of having obtained more than their fair share, but on 8 January 1942 it was the turn of a Darlington magistrate to face charges herself. Mrs Enid Stevenson of Felix House, Middleton St George, was charged with having illegally obtained butter in excess of her ration. In relation to the case, Mrs Ann Robson of Beck House, Stapleton, was also charged with having supplied the excess butter. Both women pleaded guilty to the charges. It was stated in court that Mrs Stevenson was entitled to receive 8oz of butter per week but that she had been supplied with 2lbs per week. In mitigation, both women expressed their unqualified regret, insisting that it was an innocent mistake. They claimed that before the war Mrs Robson had supplied Mrs Stevenson with 4lbs of butter per week but that this had been cut down to 2lbs after the war began. They believed that this was in line with the regulations. In an attempt to further mitigate her case, Mrs Stevenson told the court that she was a busy woman with much public and other work, that she lived in a household of seven, and had not been acquainted with the altered butter ration. She also said that, because she was not drawing any cooking fats, she thought this entitled her to a greater butter supply. These arguments made little impression upon the bench. Indeed, they seem extremely doubtful in their veracity and, clearly, the bench thought so too. Mrs Stevenson was fined £5 1s and Mrs Robson £6 1s. In summing up the case the presiding magistrate said that the bench were not happy with the explanations given by the two women. Mrs Robson, as a shop owner, could not possibly be unaware of the rationing laws and Mrs Stevenson's plea simply did not make sense.

At the start of July 1943, the same time as the Mayor was congratulating the town for its patriotic spirit in supporting the Wings for Victory campaign, the magistrates heard a case involving a Darlington haulage contractor named Horace V. Hepper, and Albert Forster Harrison, a clerk, stood accused of defrauding the War Office of the sum of £41 10s. The pair were told that the case would likely go to trial. It had all begun with the relatively trivial accusation that Mr Hepper, who was contracted to provide scavenging services for the War Office locally, had claimed for emptying fifty buckets of soil per day, when in fact he should have only been claiming for sixty buckets per week. The main villain in the case appears, in fact, to have been Mr Harrison, the clerk responsible for fuel and lighting. He had been brought up on charges the previous year but had arranged for Mr Hepper to get the local contract on the basis that he was given one-third of all the profits. Subsequent inquiry had revealed that Mr Hepper and Mr Harrison had filed 'completely fictitious and exaggerated claims' for work completed. Mr Hepper was charged with having fraudulently obtained the sum of £164 10s, but the Army and the prosecution alleged that the real total was nearer to £1,000. Mr Hepper's solicitor tried to place the blame on Mr Harrison, claiming that his client had 'been blundering on in his ignorant, uneducated fashion'.[5] Despite this, the bench found Mr Hepper guilty on six charges of false pretences, while Mr Harrison was found guilty of five charges of aiding and abetting. Mr Hepper was sentenced to three months' hard labour and Mr Harrison to six months' hard labour.

The rationing system encouraged criminality in some cases with shortages providing opportunities for the criminally inclined to exploit the massive black market for rationed and rare goods. There were profits to be made by those who could obtain an excess of foodstuffs and then illegally re-sell it. Many such crimes were small in scale but others were clearly more organised. With the crime becoming more common the local magistrates were anxious to crack down upon those brought before them. At the start of March 1944, 50-year-old Christina Melaney from Sun Street, Darlington, faced twelve charges of having obtained rationed goods through misrepresentation. The Ministry of Food alleged that the accused had, on several occasions, reported lost ration books and had obtained temporary cards. She had then drawn rations on both the cards and the lost ration books. Clearly, the accused had been encouraged in the enterprise by other members of her family as the chairman accused Melaney of being stupid and having allowed herself to be 'misled by some of your family'. The accused was fined the sum of £24 and the chairman suggested that it was up to the accused 'to see that those who got you into this trouble pay up'.[6]

Although much of the wartime crime was petty in nature and driven by shortages or by the intention to make a small profit out of wartime conditions, there had been an increase in what could only be described as organised theft. In July 1944, two women from Middleton-in-Teesdale were sentenced to four months' imprisonment after being found guilty of stealing women's and children's clothing to the value of £35 19s 5d (along with 2 guineas in costs) from Binns' Stores in Sunderland. In what the magistrate described as a 'double raid' on the store, the two women had been seen by the shop manager, Mrs Bainbridge, to be screening each other while they placed coats into their shopping bags. They left the shop, unaware that Mrs Bainbridge was following them, and went to the railway station where they placed the coats into a suitcase which they had left at the station. They then returned to the shop to steal more coats. When Mrs Bainbridge stopped them in the street and asked them quietly to come to her office they denied they had anything with them and one of the women attacked Mrs Bainbridge, kicking her in the stomach. The magistrate explained that they had been increasing fines for such offences and asked Mrs Bainbridge if this had been having any effect only to be told that it had not and incidents had in fact been increasing. Upon sentencing, the two women, Florence May Milburn (30) and Jeannie Nixon (31), cried out that they had never been to gaol before.

For some time in the run-up to the festive season of 1944, the police in the Darlington and Shildon areas had been aware of the illegal sale of bottles of spirits. In mid-December two arrests were made by Inspector Vickers of Shildon. Both of the arrested men were RCAF airmen and they confessed to having sold bottles of spirit which they had stolen from the Sergeant's mess at their airfield for the sum of £238. Following the arrests some eighty bottles of spirits were recovered from various addresses in both Darlington and Shildon. The airmen, 24-year-old Morris Urowitz and 21-year-old Nathan Thomas, were charged with having stolen spirits and cigarettes to the value of £196 2s 9d and with having taken a motor car without the owner's consent. For the latter offence both men were fined £2, while Urowitz was sentenced to three months' imprisonment and Thomas to two months.

CHAPTER 5

Industry and Agriculture

One of the key areas of employment in Darlington was railway engineering. Several firms had premises in the town and the industry was a staple for Darlington. Robert Stephenson and Hawthorns Ltd was one of the largest employers. The company built locomotives at its Darlington site and had maintained a presence in the town since 1902. Like most heavy engineering industries in the Northeast, the company had suffered during the Depression of the 1930s and business had slackened considerably. The war brought about a recovery, with orders from the government pouring in for a large number of 0-4-0 and 0-6-0 saddle tank locomotives for use in Britain's wartime industries. The Darlington Works, established in 1863 by the Stockton and Darlington Railway, was another key employer and spent much of the war building locomotives for the government. In the 1920s the hitherto rural suburb of Faverdale saw the construction of a waggon works which was to build freight waggons for the LNER (substantial housing development also began at this time). A chemical works was also built in Faverdale. The Darlington Chemical and Insulating Co. Ltd. produced a variety of goods, including magnesia coverings and 'dextramite' high temperature coverings, but during the war became involved with the production of specialised aircraft components. Other key industries in Darlington included the Whessoe Foundry Company (which specialised in equipment for the gas and oil industries as well as making linings for railway tunnels). Another key employer in Darlington was the Cleveland Bridge & Engineering Company. In addition to work on bridges, the company was involved in a variety of construction projects and was also a key steel producer during the war.

Although Darlington had a substantial rural hinterland the town itself was dependent upon heavy engineering. The town was home to a number of iron and steel foundries. The Darlington Rolling Mills Company Ltd., for example, produced a variety of products which were vital to the British war effort. The company produced metal bars and struts, steel arched roof supports, steel rails, pit props, and all manner of light steel sections. Unsurprisingly, the company played a substantial role in aircraft production during the war. The company had recently expanded and had three modern mills, while a new rivet plant was hard at work throughout the war producing rivets for the aircraft, shipbuilding, construction, locomotive and other industries.

Although Darlington was an industrialised town it did have a largely rural hinterland and agriculture still played a substantial role in the local economy. The annual sale of rams and keeping sheep was held on 22 September 1939 at the town's mart. The top price for Oxford Down rams was £13 and this was matched by a Suffolk Down shearling ram. Oxford Down shearling rams made up to £11 10s, while Suffolk Down ram lambs sold for up to £10 10s. Suffolk Border Leicester rams fetched up to £10 and Suffolk-Leicester rams £8. Among the keeping sheep, shearling gimmers made up to £3 6s 6d, half-bred ewes £2 5s and gimmer lambs £1 14s 6d.

Farmers had been ordered by the government to plough up as much of their land as was possible so that a greater amount of arable crops could be grown to feed the nation. In January 1940, however, there were complaints to Darlington Rural District Council that some farmers had been taking advantage of the order to plough up footpaths which cut across their lands. The council assured the public and notified farmers that the new laws did not allow them to plough up footpaths and rights of way but there was some disagreement, with the chairman of the committee arguing that the situation depended upon whether or not the footpaths had ever been ploughed before. It was decided that any further incidents should be brought to the attention of the council.

Darlington Rolling Mills Co. Ltd. advert from 1940. (Yorkshire Post)

The impact of the government's meat and livestock control scheme could be clearly seen at the Darlington Bank Top Cattle Mart in January. Under the scheme, the Ministry of Food became the sole buyer of all fat stock for slaughter for human consumption and there were prescribed wholesale and maximum retail prices for meat. There were far fewer people present at the mart. A number of butchers, though forbidden to buy stock for slaughter, did attend in order to see how the new scheme worked. Darlington was one of the first places where the scheme operated as it had been selected as a collecting centre. The secretary of the mart, Mr G.B. McDoric, stated to the press that the scheme had worked well in his opinion.

With large numbers of men joining the forces or being called up as members of the Reserve or Territorials, there were labour problems in some industries. There was a severe shortage of agricultural workers throughout the whole of the Northeast. The Darlington area was no different. At the beginning of May 1940 there was a rash of adverts from farmers looking for help. For example, Mr W. Thompson of West Newbiggin Farm, Sadberge, was advertising for a horseman with a strong lad for stock work to assist him, a good cottage came with the role.

Throughout 1940, Robert Stephenson and Hawthorns Ltd was still working hard on government orders but the company also manufactured four PC Class 4-6-2 locomotives for the Iraqi state railway. These locomotives were duly shipped out but only three arrived, with the fourth going down at sea when the ship it was on was sunk.

The local farmers in the Darlington area were determined to do their bit for the war effort. This meant not only growing crops for the country, but also raising money to aid the war effort. On 4 November 1940 the farmers held a gift sale of farm stock and produce in aid of the Red Cross. The sale was held at the Bank Top Auction Mart and was the largest charity sale to be held in Darlington since the First World War. A wide variety of stock was involved in the sale, including fourteen head of cattle and calves; almost sixty sheep; ten pigs; three sheepdogs; a wide variety of poultry (including chickens, ducks, and turkeys); rabbits and hares; and a wide variety of produce. The Mayor, Councillor John Dougill, opened the sale and praised the work of the Red Cross, especially in those places that had been heavily bombed. There were, the Mayor stated, those who believed that farmers were 'sometimes [a] greedy lot, but he knew different'.[1] The event had been arranged by the local branch of the National Farmers Union and Mr G. Mitchell, the chairman of the Darlington Farmers Auction Mart Co. Ltd. handed over a cheque for £100. Bidding for the early lots was brisk and the first beast offered for sale made the sum of £30 10s, while the next made £12 15s *and* a horse fetched the sum of 30 Guineas. The Croft Young Farmers' Club took advantage of the sale to donate a cheque for £100 to the Mayor in aid of the Darlington Spitfire Fund. In accepting the cheque, the Mayor commented that the fund now stood at £9,000 and he had no doubt that £10,000 would be raised before long.

The heavy industries of Darlington continued to be very busy through the early years of the war and 1942 proved particularly busy, with much of their work being war related. This was not always the case, however, and work on some civil projects continued. In 1942 the Cleveland Bridge & Engineering Company completed the construction of the Howrah Bridge over the Hooghly River in India. At the time of its construction the bridge was the third longest cantilever bridge in existence. The company was, at the time, engaged in several major engineering projects and was balancing this with a great deal of work which was war related and of great national importance. The company's expertise was particularly useful in engineering new equipment for the Royal Engineers, the Royal Navy and the RAF. Projects included the development (in collusion with other firms) of an easily laid steel runway matting system for the rapid construction of emergency airstrips. Robert Stephenson and Hawthorns Ltd were also experiencing a very busy and highly profitable war and they reported in July 1942 that their annual net profit was £18,566. The works had been 'very fully occupied' during 1942 and this profit was a reflection of that, comparing favourably with the £17,853 announced in 1941. These were just two of a number of heavy industrial concerns in the area which made an extremely valuable contribution to the war effort.

Robert Stephenson and Hawthorns Ltd were still busy with government work and the War Department as the year 1942 opened. With the great strain placed upon the railway network by the war, LNER ordered new locomotives and in January the first of a new class of 4-6-0 locomotive rolled off the production line at Darlington. Designed by Mr Edward Thompson (the Chief Mechanical Engineer of the LNER), the locomotive was of a simplicity of design which enabled ease of maintenance. Weighing in at over 123 tons, the new 'Antelope Class' was the most powerful mixed-traffic locomotive in use on the LNER. This first of its class was named Springbok. The workload of Robert Stephenson and Hawthorns Ltd increased further when the government placed an order for an additional ninety Austerity 0-6-0 Saddle Tank locomotives; all ninety of them were built during 1943.

Industrial demands on the nation's railways continued throughout 1943, with locomotives and rolling stock seeing constant work with reduced maintenance. The North British Locomotive Company and the Lancashire-based Vulcan Foundry had both received substantial orders for locomotives in 1943, with the government requesting the construction of 390 Austerity 2-8-0 locomotives and fifty Austerity 0-6-0 Saddle Tank locomotives. Partly as a result of this the company decided to expand and bought out Robert Stephenson and Hawthorns Ltd. The buy-out resulted in the Darlington works continuing its wartime work and becoming a part of the English Electric group.

The farmers surrounding Darlington and in Teesdale had been exhorted to plough up as much grassland as possible at the start of the war, but in the last two years the focus changed and farmers were being urged to produce more livestock. As a result, grassland was now needed again and farming methods were changing. The government, however, remained determined to aid farmers as much as possible. On the evening of 15 February 1945, a meeting was held at The George

Hotel, Piercebridge, under the auspices of the Durham War Agricultural Committee. The key speaker at the meeting was Mr William Davies of the Ministry of Agriculture (MoAg) Grassland Improvement Station and his subject was to be 'the use of the long duration ley'. The use of ley farming techniques was being encouraged by some within the MoAg. The technique involved using a piece of land to grow grains for several seasons followed by leaving it fallow and utilising it for either hay production or pasture for several more seasons before once again ploughing the land up and reusing it to grow a cash crop. The technique allowed the land to recover from the intensive drain of nutrients involved in growing grain crops but had been uncommon before the war as many farmers saw it as being unprofitable in the short term.

CHAPTER 6

The Darlington Spitfire

By the summer of 1940 the Battle of Britain was raging and the people of Darlington had recently witnessed part of the battle directly above their heads when RAF Fighter Command had repulsed an attempted raid on the Northeast. It is therefore unsurprising that the Spitfire funds being undertaken by many communities found great popularity in the area. On 20 September, two directors of the engineering firm Henry Williams, Ltd made a very substantial and generous donation of £5,000 to the fund.[1] In an accompanying letter, Mr Owen Williams explained how he and his brother Denis had decided some time previously to each donate £2,500 to a Spitfire fund but had been prevented from doing so by the demands of their work, which included travelling for vital war work. The two directors no longer lived in Darlington and had only recently become aware of the town's own fund, but because of their longstanding connection with the town, had decided that Darlington's fund would be the most suitable for their donation. Mr Williams concluded his letter by expressing the hope that the donation would enable Darlington to keep pace with other communities and would inspire others to contribute and pay tribute to 'the magnificent and epic achievements of our gallant fighter and bomber crews'.

There were in fact two Darlington Spitfires. The first had been purchased by the chairman and managing director of Henry Williams Ltd, but the second and most famous one had been purchased with the £5,082 which was promised and subsequently donated by the people of Darlington.

Darlington was among many communities that took the decision to purchase their own iconic Spitfire fighter aircraft which would proudly bear the name of the town into battle. The 'Darlington Spitfire', built by Vickers-Armstrong, was part of a batch ordered in March 1940. Although the plane was originally ordered as a MkI Spitfire, rapid developments saw the batch completed as Mark VBs. The Darlington Spitfire was numbered W3320 and had the name 'Darlington' painted below the cockpit.

Delivered to 9 Maintenance Unit (MU) in early June, the Darlington Spitfire remained at the MU for a month before it was assigned to 92 (East India) Squadron at RAF Biggin Hill. The Darlington Spitfire was immediately adopted by Sergeant Donald Kingaby, DFM, an ace with fifteen victories and named by the press as the '109 specialist' for his skill in shooting down Me109s. In the same month that the Darlington Spitfire arrived at 92 Squadron, Sergeant Kingaby was awarded a bar to his DFM.

The Darlington Spitfire continued to serve throughout the summer. On 7 August 1941, Kingaby, flying the Darlington Spitfire on a Circus operation (code for the escorting of short-range bombing operations against targets in France or the Low Countries. The 'Circus' consisted of several squadrons of fighters) escorting British bombers over France, claimed one Me109 damaged and one Me109 probably destroyed. Two days later, Kingaby and the Darlington Spitfire claimed their first definite victory. On another sweep over France Kingaby destroyed an Me109 and claimed another as probably destroyed.

At the end of September 1941, 92 Squadron was moved to RAF Gravesend and on a sweep on the first day of October, Kingaby, now a Flight Sergeant, and the Darlington Spitfire claimed yet another Me109 destroyed and another probable. Two days later, Kingaby and his beloved Spitfire were on another Circus operation. On this occasion the Darlington Spitfire was giving him trouble. An electrical fault had knocked out his wireless telephone and his reflector gunsight. This put him at a serious disadvantage during the dogfight which developed. Kingaby spotted a gaggle of Me109s which were about to bounce his squadron, but was unable to warn his comrades due to his w/t (wireless/telephone) being inoperable. Instead he attacked the Me109s.

Surrounded by six or seven of them, he found glycol leaking into his cockpit and decided to abandon the sortie and attempt to return to base. He was pursued by seven Me109s, but all but one gave up the chase. This determined Me109 quickly closed with the Darlington Spitfire and Kingaby turned and engaged his foe. Following a turning fight, Kingaby gained the upper hand and the Me109 dived to sea level to try to escape the British ace but Kingaby hit the Me109 with a long burst and it crashed into the sea. Upon his return to base the relieved pilot discovered that the glycol had not been a result of damage to the Darlington Spitfire, but was the result of a faulty windscreen anti-freeze device.

Although Kingaby and several other pilots scored well, casualties in 92 Squadron were high and on 20 October the squadron was moved north from Gravesend to Lincolnshire, out of the front line. Flight Sergeant Kingaby left the squadron in early November, after having been awarded a second bar to his DFM.[2] Almost as if mourning the loss of her favoured pilot, the Darlington Spitfire departed the squadron on 11 November when she was sent to 24 MU.

As we have seen, the Darlington Spitfire had experienced an action-packed 1941 which ended with the aircraft being posted to 24 MU, but 1942 proved to be a very different year for the aircraft. On 1 March she was allocated to 54 Squadron but there was little prospect of action as the squadron was, at the time, based in the far north of Scotland at RAF Castletown. Morale was poor in the squadron as it felt like it had been forgotten about. Furthermore, there had been a series of flying accidents and on 19 April the Darlington Spitfire fell victim to this plague of accidents. On the day in question she was being flown by Sergeant le Peutrec, one of three Free French pilots on the squadron, but he unfortunately managed to crash the Spitfire while attempting to land. After a series of assessments and repairs, the Darlington Spitfire was sent to 12 MU where she appears to have been somewhat forgotten about.

Having languished at 12 MU for eight months the Darlington Spitfire resumed operational life when she was allocated to 118 Squadron at RAF Coltishall, Norfolk. The Darlington Spitfire once again had a regular pilot. Pilot Officer R.J. Flight was a recent arrival on the squadron but had just completed a fighter leader's course and so was an experienced pilot. 118 Squadron flew a great deal of close escort operations in which it protected Allied bombers, and so the Darlington Spitfire had long-range tanks fitted. Many of these missions were to escort the Beaufighters of the various anti-shipping strike wings and July saw the Darlington Spitfire and 118 Squadron very active on a variety of anti-shipping tasks and escort operations, largely off the coast of Norway. On 27 July the squadron was escorting B-25 Mitchell bombers which were to bomb Schiphol airfield. The Luftwaffe responded in force and 118 squadron scored two victories, including a shared 'probable' for Pilot Officer Flight and the Darlington Spitfire.

August 1943 continued to be busy for 118 Squadron and the Darlington Spitfire, with further escort operations and 'Jim Crow' anti-shipping reconnaissance operations, but there was little action involving the enemy and in mid-August 1943 the squadron moved south to RAF Westhampnett, nr Chichester. Several escort operations were carried out, but the stay at Westhampnett lasted just a week before the squadron was relocated to Merston in West Sussex.

The Darlington Spitfire had been in the thick of the action during August and September, being involved in a number of escort operations, but without further victories. On 15 September the wing to which 118 Squadron belonged engaged Fw190s when it escorted another bomber mission. On this occasion the Darlington Spitfire was being flown by Flight Lieutenant A. Drew. The operation saw Flying Officer Flight (who, as a Pilot Officer, had previously flown the Darlington Spitfire on occasion) forced to bale out after his engine caught fire, he spent the rest of the war as a PoW. Just days later, the Darlington Spitfire (along with all of 118 Squadron's aircraft) was swapped with those of 64 Squadron because 118 Squadron moved north to Scotland while 64 Squadron remained at West Malling in Kent, flying similar operations.

On 24 September 1943, 64 Squadron, including the Darlington Spitfire, were escorting a group of Marauder bombers over Evereux. The Darlington Spitfire was being flown by an American pilot serving in the RAF, Flying Officer J.W. Harder. The section in which Flying Officer Harder flew claimed a shared victory over an Me109, but Harder was forced to put down at RAF Friston, near Beachy Head, following engine trouble on return. Shortly afterward 64 Squadron was posted to RAF Coltishall. It would be a month before the Darlington Spitfire was ready to fly on operations again.

The RAF continued to attract attention. The Darlington Spitfire had gained itself another regular pilot when Flight Sergeant J.D.H. Duncan took her over but the first months of 1944 had been very quiet ones. This changed when the squadron moved to the West Country at the end of May, but although a high number of operations were flown, there was little opportunity to engage the enemy. 64 Squadron provided low beach cover over Omaha Beach during D-Day. On 16 June the Darlington Spitfire lost another regular pilot when Flight Sergeant Duncan was killed when he was hit by flak over St Lo. The Darlington Spitfire was unserviceable for most of June and she left the squadron on 3 July as the Spitfire Vs were replaced with Spitfire IXs. The Darlington Spitfire was posted across the aerodrome to the neighbouring 611 Squadron, but was transferred to 9 MU just a couple of weeks later as 611 also re-equipped.

On 5 October the Darlington Spitfire joined her sixth and final operational squadron. 63 Squadron was tasked with flying support operations for supply and paratrooper-carrying aircraft and frequently engaged in the silencing of anti-aircraft positions. On 12 October the Darlington Spitfire provided escort to bombers attacking gun positions near to Breskens on the Dutch coast with Flight Lieutenant J.D. Scholey flying her.

On 28 October the Darlington Spitfire flew a similar operation over Walcheren. Once again, Flight Lieutenant J.D. Scholey was at the controls. On that same evening, however, a Spitfire from 310 (Czechoslovakia) Squadron ran into the Darlington Spitfire in a landing accident and she was damaged. This effectively put the well-travelled Darlington Spitfire out of the war.

It is not known where the Darlington Spitfire met her eventual end, but it seems likely that she was transferred to 41 OTU when 63 Squadron was disbanded in January. It is known that the Darlington Spitfire was struck off charge on 21 June 1947.[3] The Darlington Spitfire had flown with the RAF during three-and-a-half years of the war. During that time she had served with no fewer than six squadrons, had amassed at least 161 operational sorties and had scored three confirmed victories, three-and-a-half probables and one damaged. All of these victories, barring the shared probable, had come at the hands of noted ace Donald Kingaby.

CHAPTER 7

RAF Middleton St George

The village of Middleton St George lies approximately two miles from Darlington and when RAF Middleton St George was declared operational in January 1940 it became the most northerly Bomber Command base in the country and the nearest to Darlington. The station was to remain a bomber base throughout the war. At first allocated to 4 Group, the base had to wait several months before its first operational squadron arrived, but for bomber crews released from duty, Darlington became a familiar location. Many wartime airmen stationed there spent their off-duty hours in the pubs, dancehalls and cinemas of Darlington, and many Darlington families forged bonds with the airmen from the nearby station.

These bonds, formed with many local families, often proved to be fleeting and on many occasions ended in tragic circumstances with the airmen either failing to return from operations or being posted away. The sacrifices that were very obviously being made by the airmen played a large role in earning the respect and often love of local people.

On 7 April 1940, RAF Middleton St George received its first operational squadron when the Armstrong Whitworth Whitley Vs of 78 Squadron arrived. At the time of its arrival 78 Squadron was already experienced and 78 Squadron was thrown straight into the action following its arrival at Middleton St George. On the night of 7/8 April the squadron christened its new airfield by sending a number of aircraft to attack the German city of Kiel, all returned safely. On the night of 3/4 May the squadron suffered its first loss when the aircraft of Sergeant L. Hatcher had to be abandoned upon return to Britain due to lack of fuel and wireless failure. Five nights later the squadron suffered its first failure to return when Sergeant L. Thorpe and his crew were lost aboard Whitley V (T4147, EY-D) on an operation to Bremen. A further two aircraft were lost, with no survivors, before the end of May.

The bomber offensive was being expanded and on 4 June 1941 the resident 78 Squadron was joined at Middleton St George by 76 Squadron with the new four-engine Handley Page Halifax heavy bomber. 76 Squadron was given a few days to settle in before it mounted its first operation from its new base on the night of 12/13 June. This was a small attack on the German Huls Chemical Works, undertaken by just eleven Halifaxes and seven Short Stirlings. All of 76 Squadron's aircraft returned safely. It was not long, however, before the squadron suffered its first loss, not on a mission but during a training exercise. The accident happened in good weather and visibility, when Pilot Officer A.E. Lewin was carrying out practice circuits and landings in Halifax I (L9514). During one landing the Halifax swung off the runway and the undercarriage collapsed. There were no serious injuries but the Halifax was so badly damaged that it was later struck off charge and scrapped.

The Whitleys of 78 Squadron suffered badly throughout 1941, losing four aircraft in June alone. 76 Squadron, however, suffered its first operational loss of a Halifax aircraft on the night of 23/24 June when the Halifax I (L9492) flown by Pilot Officer W.K. Stobbs failed to return from an operation to Kiel.[1]

By mid-1941 the people of Darlington had become used to the airmen of 76 and 78 Squadrons visiting their town – when they were not flying on operations – and the exploits of the squadrons was followed keenly (as much as censorship allowed).

On the night of 12/13 August 1941 the target was Berlin; the raid was to result in disheartening losses for 78 Squadron with two of its Halifaxes failing to return. Among them was the aircraft and crew of the popular Flight Lieutenant Christopher Cheshire, the brother of Leonard Cheshire, VC. Flight Lieutenant Cheshire's aircraft was shot down by flak, but Cheshire and four of his crew survived, although two air gunners were killed. The horrors of the war were brought home to Middleton St George at the end of this raid when a third Halifax crashed at 5.25am on approach to base. The crew of Halifax I (L9562), piloted by Sergeant J. McHale, were all killed in the crash.[2]

Middleton St George became slightly less crowded on 20 October when 78 Squadron moved to nearby RAF Croft from where it carried on the war with its aging Whitleys. For 76 Squadron, however, the war continued as normal from Middleton St George and the non-operational 1516 Beam Approach Training Flight (BATF) joined 76 Squadron at the base in November.[3] Throughout the period, the squadron continued regular operations against Germany and suffered a steady rate of losses.

With ever-increasing numbers of the four-engine heavy bombers being brought into service it became evident that many crews were being lost in needless accidents through unfamiliarity with the newer, more complex, aircraft which were a technological step up from the aircraft with which squadrons had begun the war. As a result, many squadrons set up their own Conversion Flights (CF). In January 1942, 76 Squadron at Middleton St George followed suit and 76 CF came into existence. The CFs were an emergency measure and by the end of the year they would be replaced by specialised Heavy Conversion Units (HCU) with their own bases.

During the summer there were further changes at RAF Middleton St George. 78 Squadron, now re-equipped with the Halifax II, had returned to Middleton St George on 10 June 1942, while 76 Squadron remained at the base and also sent some detachments to the Middle East. The airfield became even more crowded when they were joined by the Halifaxes of 78 CU. 1516 BATF and 76 Squadron both suffered a loss on 26 June as the result of a collision between an Airspeed Oxford (V4140) of 1516 BATF and a 76 Squadron Halifax II (W7661). Both aircraft crashed as a result of the collision and all aboard were killed. This was a tragic reminder of the dangers of flying in the sometimes overcrowded skies above wartime Britain.

The two Halifax squadrons which were based at Middleton St George had notable commanding officers through the summer of 1942. 78 Squadron was commanded by Wing Commander J.B. Tait (known as Willy), DSO, DFC, while 76 Squadron was commanded by Wing Commander Leonard Cheshire, VC, DSO (and two bars), DFC. Both men would go on to become legends in Bomber Command and both would go on to survive the war having commanded the elite 617 Squadron.

In September 1942 there was an upheaval at Middleton St George which resulted in both 76 and 78 Squadrons (and their CUs) being posted elsewhere. The change came about due to the decision to organise an entire new group in Bomber Command. 6 (RCAF) Group was formed from squadrons drawn from the RCAF and had a Canadian commanding officer in Air Vice-Marshal G. Brookes (a Yorkshire-born Canadian). Middleton St George had been assigned to the new formation. The creation of 6 Group meant that the squadrons of 4 Group which had been based in and around North Yorkshire and County Durham were moved to other bases (still largely in North Yorkshire) while the Canadians took over their old airfields (which were often pre-war and more comfortable than the ones which the 4 Group squadrons moved to).

The first RCAF squadron arrived at Middleton St George on 15 October 1942 when 420 (Snowy Owl) Squadron, RCAF, landed at the base with its Wellington IIIs. The Canadian squadrons often had fanciful and poetic names attached to them. Often these were creatures of their homeland but others were more fanciful. The squadron launched its first raid from Middleton St George on the night that it arrived. The target was Cologne and 420 Squadron lost one of its Wellingtons when X3808 with Flight Sergeant L.E. White, RCAF, and his crew failed to return.

On 10 November a second RCAF squadron arrived at Middleton St George. 419 (Moose) Squadron brought the familiar sight of the Halifax, with which it had just been equipped, back to the station when it arrived. Once again the airfield was to play host to two bomber squadrons. It would take some time for the groups to become operational but in the meantime extensive training was undertaken.

On the first day of 1943 6 (RCAF) Group became operational and it wasn't long before Middleton St George witnessed its first incident of the year. On 8 January a Wellington III (BJ604, ZL-A) of 427 Squadron attempted to land at the airfield but overshot the runway and came to rest on the nearby Darlington-Eaglescliffe railway line. The crew all managed to scramble clear but a train then hit the wreckage; one person on the train was killed and another injured.

When Arthur Harris launched his main offensive with a raid on Essen, in what would become known as the Battle of the Ruhr, on the night of 5/6 March the Middleton St George squadrons both participated. Two aircraft from the base failed to return from the operation. 420 Squadron lost P/O Graham and his crew while 419 Squadron lost Sgt L. Bakewell and his crew.

428 (Ghost) Squadron, RCAF, arrived at Middleton in June 1943. On 19/20 June 428 Squadron joined 419 Squadron on its first raid from Middleton St George with a raid on Le Creusot in France. This was an unusual raid in that it was carried out at low level; but it was largely unsuccessful, although all of Middleton's aircraft returned.

The newly arrived 428 Squadron suffered its first casualty when one of its most experienced captains failed to return from Gelsenkirchen on 9/10 July. Halifax V (DK229, NA-W) and the crew of Squadron Leader F.H. Bowden, DFC and Bar, failed to return. Squadron Leader Bowden was one of the squadron's flight commanders and was nearing the end of his second operational tour. The Halifax was hit by flak in the vicinity of Cologne and Squadron Leader Bowden ordered the crew to abandon while he held the aircraft steady. All of the crew managed to bale out, but Squadron Leader Bowden paid the price that many bomber pilots paid in remaining at his post until his crew had baled out of the aircraft and was killed when the bomber crashed.

By now the Battle of the Ruhr was reaching its conclusion but Harris sent a force on a highly successful attack on Aachen on 13/14 July 1943. Enemy night fighter activity was intense and twenty-three bombers failed to return. Three Halifaxes from 428 Squadron failed to return to Middleton St George. Flight Lieutenant G. Weeks, RCAF, and his crew were shot down by a night fighter in Halifax V (DK228, NA-D); Halifax V (DK257, NA-Q) with Flight Lieutenant D.S. Moran, RCAF, and crew also fell victim to a night fighter; and Pilot Officer W.D.F. Ross, RCAF, and his crew in Halifax V (ED209, NA-C) were lost to flak. One aircraft from 419 Squadron failed to return. Halifax II (BB323, VR-R) with the American 2nd Lieutenant B.J.J. Furey at the controls, was attacked by a night fighter whose fire killed the rear gunner. The night fighter then shot down the Halifax but the remainder of the crew were able to bale out.

Although the vast majority of Bomber Command raids were on city or area targets the command did occasionally undertake precision raids on specific targets. The Peenemunde raid on 17/18 August was one such raid. The attack was made on the V-Rocket development and testing site on the Baltic island of Peenemunde and was made in full moonlight conditions. The successful raid proved to be disastrous for 6 Group. The final wave of bombers (made up of aircraft from 5 and 6 Groups) fell victim to night fighter attacks and the Canadians lost twelve of their aircraft from just 57 on the operation. Six aircraft failed to return to Middleton St George that night, three from each squadron. The heavier casualties that were being suffered were no secret to the people of Darlington. Many had formed friendships with the men serving in the two squadrons at Middleton St George and they were painfully aware that such friendships often proved to be fleeting as bomber crews failed to return from operations. The loss of aircrew during this period of intense operations not only placed a strain on the airmen but also affected the morale of the civilians in communities such as Darlington and the surrounding areas which had welcomed the airmen and developed friendships with many of them.

Wing Commander G. McMurdy, RCAF, took over the command of 419 Squadron on 11 October 1943. Squadron commanders flew on fewer operations than other aircrew but were still expected to fly a full tour of operations. One role of the commander of a squadron was to provide leadership and reassurance to inexperienced crews and many elected to fly on operations with such crews in order to bolster their confidence. On 22/23 October a raid on Kassel took place. Two aircraft failed to return to Middleton St George, one from each squadron. For Wing Commander McMurdy this was his first and last operation with the squadron. Halifax II (JD382, VR-A) was shot down by a night fighter and five of the eight crew were killed, including Wing Commander McMurdy.

Since January 1943 the airmen of 6 (RCAF) Group, Bomber Command, had been flying on operations from their airfields in North Yorkshire. The northernmost of these airfields was that of RAF Middleton St George, but on 31 May 1945 the Lancaster bombers of 428 (Ghost) Squadron, RCAF, flew off from their wartime airfield for the final time. The fifteen Lancasters took off, each with their seven-man crews along with two ground staff passengers whose services were required back in Canada.

428 Squadron was chosen as the first of the 6 Group squadrons to depart Britain for home. The airmen were, of course, excited and pleased to be going home but there was also a strong sense of regret over the breaking of wartime associations with local people. Many a 428 Squadron crew had formed friendships with people in the village of Middleton St George or from other nearby communities. Many of the aircrew visited Darlington during stand-down periods. Although

a Canadian squadron there had also been numbers of British airmen on the squadron too and for these men the departure was bittersweet. The flight engineers were, in the main, British, as were some of the groundcrew and WAAFs. Another separation, although this time temporary, involved the twenty-five to thirty Canadian airmen who had married English women. The wives of these airmen were to follow them to Canada at the earliest opportunity.

The guest of honour at the departing ceremony was Air Chief Marshal Sir Arthur Harris. The wartime commander of Bomber Command had flown north especially to mark the occasion and he praised 6 Group and the Canadian crews in other squadrons as being among the very best. Sir Arthur completed his speech by telling the airmen that when asked what they had done in the war they could answer, 'without blushing. I won it. You won't be very far from the truth.' The Mayor of

Canadian airmen wave goodbye prior to departing Middleton St George.
(The Yorkshire Post)

*Sir Arthur Harris addresses
428 Squadron before their
departure.* (The Yorkshire Post)

Darlington and various other local dignitaries were also in attendance
for the ceremony, representing the people of the area, many of whom
had forged close bonds with various airmen.

  As the aircraft departed at intervals of one minute, they were cheered
on their way by the groundcrew and a group of WAAFs. The 6 Group
band was also present but many of the tunes were drowned out by the
roaring Merlin engines. The Lancasters then circled their former base
until all were aloft. The final Lancaster to lift off dipped its wings in
salute as the crew fired green and red flares. The Canadian Lancasters
made for a colourful sight with each one being named and having nose
art present. Among the names were 'Fearless Fox', 'Don't Panic' and
'Fighting Cock'. Some of the Lancasters were veterans, having flown
many operations against the Reich; 'Malton Mike', however, was a
relatively new aircraft. This was the 300th Lancaster to have been built
in Canada and had arrived on the squadron just in time to take part in
its last few operations.

CHAPTER 8

Darlington Sailors

The news that the battleship HMS *Royal Oak* had been sunk while at anchor in the allegedly impregnable fleet berth at Scapa Flow on 14 October sent shockwaves through Britain and caused considerable anxiety in Darlington, because several young sailors were serving aboard the ship. The *Royal Oak* had a very large number of boy-sailors, under the age of 18, aboard at the time of her sinking and 134 of these youngsters were lost with the ship. Three of those lost were from Darlington. Boy 1st Class Joseph Wilkinson (16) of Geneva Road, Darlington, had written home to his mother just two days before his death. In his letter he had been uncomplaining and had asked for a parcel of some minor comforts which his mother had immediately sent, but her son would never receive the parcel. Boy 1st Class Jack Douglas Gowan (16) of Bright Street had also gone down with the aging battleship. The third Darlington casualty aboard HMS *Royal Oak* was 22-year-old Able Seaman George Raymond Simpson of Victoria Road. Able Seaman Simpson was a former pupil at St John's School and Darlington Eastbourne Senior School and had been in the Royal Navy for six years.[1] Better news was received by the families of Boy 1st Class Gordon Edward Dove (16) and Assistant Cook Thomas William Taylor (19) who had both been saved from the disaster. Boy 1st Class Dove had been in the Royal Navy since the age of 14, while Assistant Cook Taylor had only served since November 1938.

With German forces having quickly overrun Denmark and large parts of Norway, the British and French agreed to land forces in Norway in order to oppose this invasion and hopefully throw the German forces back. Once again, though, the Allies were shown to be hopelessly optimistic about the challenges which faced them. The disastrous

Norwegian campaign, launched on 8 April 1940, saw ill-prepared and poorly equipped troops landed with little plan to stem the German invasion, and ended just two months later with the ignominious evacuation of the Allied forces.

The failed campaign, which saw the death of at least one Darlington sailor, came as a fearsome blow to morale in Britain and was partly responsible for the collapse of the Chamberlain government. Press reports as the campaign was ongoing sought to reassure people that it was proceeding well but then came complete collapse and a mass evacuation. Able Seaman Thomas William Bulmer (24) was killed when a bomb hit the anti-aircraft cruiser HMS *Curacoa* while she was attempting to provide protection to the British beachhead at Andalsnes.[2] Eight of the cruiser's crew were killed in the attack. Able Seaman Bulmer had married in September 1939 when on leave in London. His widow, Phylis, was from Ardrossan.

One of the problems facing the Allies as they attempted to evacuate ground forces from Norway was the lack of aerial support which was available. This led to the Admiralty dispatching two aircraft carriers, HMS *Ark Royal* and HMS *Glorious,* to the Norwegian coast. Both aircraft carriers had previously supported Norwegian operations earlier in the campaign. The campaign was a fractious one and revealed tensions between the British and the French and in the British command structures. On 8 June the commanding officer of HMS *Glorious* received permission to return to Britain in order to court-martial the Commander (Air) who had refused to launch an attack on several ground targets as he claimed they were poorly defined and the aircraft available were unsuitable for such attacks. In company with two destroyers, HMS *Acasta* and HMS *Ardent,* the old carrier, which had been converted from a First World War battlecruiser, set sail for the Clyde. The three ships were sighted and engaged by two German battleships. HMS *Ardent* was quickly sunk with only one survivor while, after a short engagement, both HMS *Glorious* and HMS *Acasta* were also sunk.

HMS *Glorious* seems to have been completely unready for action. She had no aircraft available for immediate launch, no standing air patrol and, inexplicably, remained on her course after sending HMS *Ardent* to identify the closing battleships. The carrier was lost, along with 1,207 men. There were at least two Darlington sailors among the dead. Petty Officer Telegraphist Thomas Michael Slater was a 26-year-old married man serving aboard the *Glorious* and is commemorated on the Portsmouth Naval Memorial. Leading Signalman Richard Danby Barrow (21) was lost aboard HMS *Ardent* and is commemorated on the Plymouth Naval Memorial.

Following the fall of Norway, the Germans launched their expected invasion of France and the Low Countries on 10 May 1940. The Allies were quickly forced onto the defensive and British forces, despite courageous resistance, were outflanked and repeatedly forced to retreat. It quickly became clear that for the majority of the British Expeditionary Force (BEF) a hasty retreat to the port of Dunkirk was the only way in which they might be evacuated as French resistance crumbled. As the British soldiers (along with thousands of French soldiers) assembled on the beaches at Dunkirk the Royal Navy mounted a massive and dangerous ad hoc evacuation to salvage the situation as far as possible and prevent total disaster.

On 1 June and towards the end of the Dunkirk evacuation the anti-submarine warfare trawler HMT *Stella Dorado* was attacked by a German motor-torpedo boat (MTB) and sunk by a torpedo with the loss of all hands as she helped evacuate troops. Among her crew was Stoker 2nd Class Hercules Jenkinson, a 25-year-old Darlington man. Stoker Jenkinson is commemorated on the Lowestoft Naval Memorial.

With news of Darlington men being killed during the fall of France and the Dunkirk evacuation, the family of Marine William Wilfred Taylor might have been shocked to receive notice of his death because he was serving aboard HMS *Rodney* in Orkney. How the 19-year-old Marine met his end is something of a mystery.

Local press reports stated that he had died of wounds received on active service, so it is possible that he may have been victim of the probing air raids that were made on Scapa Flow. Prior to his death, Marine Taylor had been a member of the Salvation Army in his hometown.

Although much public attention focused upon the battle in France and over Britain during 1940, other campaigns continued. Amongst these was the campaign against the powerful Italian Navy in the Mediterranean. The Royal Navy's Mediterranean Fleet was stretched thin in contesting the sea with the Italians and their German allies and protecting the convoys which were vital for the resupply of both Malta and North Africa. On 8 October 1940 the Mediterranean Fleet had put to sea to protect two convoys and to try to bring the Italians to battle. They largely failed in the latter aim but the two convoys were successfully protected and an aerial raid (with aircraft from HMS *Illustrious*) on the island of Leros was made which damaged and destroyed a number of positions. On 14 October the light cruiser HMS *Liverpool* and several other escorts were returning to base when the *Liverpool* was attacked by Italian torpedo-bombers. HMS *Liverpool* was hit by a torpedo and a fuel leak led to a huge explosion which seriously damaged the ship, including compromising the integrity of the ship's bow. A number of sailors were injured or killed in the initial explosion. The cruiser was taken under tow, but on 15 October the bow became detached. HMS *Liverpool*, still under tow, reached Alexandria on 16 October and the more badly injured were taken to hospital. Among the most serious cases was 19-year-old Signalman Cyril Cowley, the son of Thomas and Elizabeth Cowley of Darlington. Sadly, the young seaman died of his injuries on 18 October and was subsequently buried at Alexandria (Chatby) Military and War Memorial Cemetery.[3]

On the same day that HMS *Liverpool* was torpedoed, another Darlington sailor lost his life in action. Engine Room Artificer 2nd Class Henry Guy (29) was serving aboard the submarine HMS

Triad in the Mediterranean when she was apparently engaged and sunk by an Italian submarine. The *Triad* was lost with all hands.[4]

The men of the Merchant Navy faced terrible hardships and dangers during the course of the war. The people of the east coast were used to hearing battles out at sea and seeing survivors brought ashore. Captain Thomas William Smith of Killerby, Piercebridge, was one of a number of Merchant Navy officers who, in August 1941, were commended for their brave conduct when encountering the enemy. Captain Smith had been at sea since he was a boy and had been employed for many years by the Constantine Shipping Line of Middlesbrough. He was commended for his conduct in picking up twenty-eight survivors following an E-boat attack on the convoy of which he was a part.

Many liners and other vessels were pressed into naval service during the war. The five Lady Class liners of the Canadian National Steamship Company were among those pressed into service. On the morning of 19 January 1942 the RMS *Lady Hawkins* was steaming off Cape

HMS Triad. (Public Domain)

The repaired HMS Liverpool *in 1942.* (Public Domain)

Hatteras on a voyage from Montreal to Bermuda and the Caribbean. On board the liner were 213 passengers and 107 crew, and she was carrying almost 3,000 tons of mixed cargo. The liner was unescorted and was zig-zagging to make herself a harder target, but at 7.43am she was hit by two torpedoes and sank within half an hour. There were only 71 survivors with 251 losing their lives. Many of the passengers aboard the RMS *Lady Hawkins* were Royal Navy personnel and among them was a 19-year-old Darlington man, Ordinary Seaman Edward Bainbridge Jackson.[5]

With the Allies keen to offer as much support as possible to Russia, a great deal of Royal Navy assets were devoted to escort work for the Arctic Convoys which often put into Murmansk. On 17 January 1942 the Tribal Class destroyer HMS *Matabele* was acting as escort along with one of her sister ships and the cruiser HMS *Trinidad* when their convoy came under attack by *U-454*. A Russian trawler was sunk and then a merchant ship damaged. The stricken merchantman was taken under tow by a Royal Navy minesweeper and HMS *Matabele* was detached to provide escort as the convoy steamed ahead. *U-454* manoeuvred into position and a single torpedo struck the destroyer, causing a magazine to explode. The destroyer sank in just two minutes and many men were forced to jump into the freezing sea. Many of the crew were killed when the ship's depth charges exploded as she sank and others were killed in the freezing temperatures. Only two men survived from the crew. Ordinary Seaman John Oldfield (19) of Darlington was among the crewmen who did not survive the disaster.[6]

A number of Darlington men had found pre-war employment in the fishing industry and many of these men were called into service as members of the Royal Naval Reserve (RNR). Other young men joined

HMS Matabele. (Public Domain)

the Royal Navy and ended up serving in the Patrol Service aboard smaller vessels. Seaman Reginald Rea was one such Darlington man. A married 25-year-old, in 1942 he was serving aboard the anti-submarine trawler HMS *Notts County*. Shortly after midnight on 9 March the trawler was off Iceland in the company of HMS *Angle* when she was struck by a torpedo fired from *U-701*. The trawler quickly settled and sunk with only one survivor picked up from the forty-two-man crew.[7]

Less than a week after Seaman Rea was killed another Darlington seaman lost his life. Able Seaman John Johnson (22) was a crewmember aboard HMS *Vortigern*. The destroyer was a First World War veteran of the V&W Class and had been refitted for service during the current conflict. In September 1941 she had been refitted as a short-range escort and on 15 March she was escorting a south-bound convoy off the east coast when she was torpedoed by an E-boat; 147 of her crew lost their lives with only twelve survivors.[8]

The destroyer HMS *Jaguar* led an action-packed war, taking part in east-coast convoys, the Dunkirk evacuation, Operation Medium, Operation Abstention and the Battle of Cape Matapan. On 26 March 1942 she was off Sidi Barrani, Egypt, when she was hit and sunk by two torpedoes fired from *U-652*; 193 of her crew were lost with just fifty-three survivors. Two Darlington men were among the lost crew. Leading Writer Thomas Ernest Tate (21) and Ordinary Artificer 4th Class Robert Downing (25) are both commemorated on the Portsmouth Naval Memorial.

As the siege of Malta ground on, the situation grew increasingly desperate and Operation Pedestal was launched on 3 August 1942 to force through a much-needed convoy to the island. The convoy consisted of fourteen merchants but was escorted by an unprecedented number of warships, including several aircraft carriers. Among these was HMS *Indomitable*. On 12 August the carrier was hit by two 500lb bombs dropped by German dive-bombers and damaged by several near-misses. HMS *Indomitable* caught fire when a 500lb bomb

HMS Vortigern *during the First World War.* (Public Domain)

penetrated the unarmoured part of the flight deck. Several of the crew were killed, including Leading Writer William Barnett Richardson (23) of Darlington.

By 1940 Britain had been desperate to obtain more light warships to act as convoy escorts and the Lend-lease agreement with America enabled the transfer of several older American vessels to the Royal Navy. Among these vessels was the Lake Class cutter *Sebago*, which had formerly served with the US Coast Guard. Renamed the HMS *Walney* the cutter served as an escort in the Atlantic. With the Allies planning a landing in North Africa, codenamed Operation Torch, the plans for HMS *Walney* changed and she was prepared for special duties – breaking into Oran harbour, in north-west Algeria. The action, on 8 October 1942, went badly with *Walney* coming under very heavy fire and, although she did ram the outer and inner booms, she was sunk with the loss of all but fourteen of her crew. Most of the 235 US troops aboard were also killed. Darlington-born Chief Engine Room Artificer Richard Longbone (32) was among the lost crew.[9]

HMS Indomitable *on fire after being hit on 12 August.* (Public Domain)

Just four days later another Darlington sailor was killed when HMS *Marne*, acting as an escort as part of Operation Torch, had her stern blown off by a torpedo. Several of HMS *Marne's* crew were killed in the attack. The stricken destroyer was towed into Gibraltar for repairs. Among those who had been killed was Able Seaman Dudley Marcus Bath (31).[10]

One of the most dangerous roles that could be undertaken by members of the Royal Navy was service aboard a submarine. Royal Navy submarines in the Mediterranean were constantly harassing the efforts to provide supplies to, or evacuate troops from, the German positions in Tunisia. In March, the submarine HMS *Thunderbolt* was lost in the Mediterranean. *Thunderbolt* had in fact once been HMS *Thetis*, but *Thetis* had been accidentally sunk with all hands in 1939 while on sea-trials. An inquiry showed that an inner torpedo hatch had been mistakenly opened and the submarine had quickly flooded;

HMS Marne *after having her stern blown off.* (Public Domain)

HMS Walney *in RN service.* (Public Domain)

it was subsequently recovered, renamed and recommissioned. As *Thunderbolt*, the vessel had a successful career against Italian forces in the Mediterranean, but on 14 March, following a successful attack on an Italian convoy, she was sunk by depth charges from an Italian warship. Once again, the submarine was lost with all hands. Among the crew was Lieutenant Edmund Philip Maw (28) from Darlington.[11]

On 6 September 1943 a further two Darlington sailors lost their lives to a U-Boat attack. HMS *Puckeridge*, a Hunt-Class destroyer, was forty miles off Gibraltar when she was hit by two torpedoes fired by *U-617*. The torpedoes caused the aft magazine to detonate and the destroyer sank in eight minutes. Despite this, 129 men of the 191-strong crew survived. Among the sixty-two victims were two 20-year-old Darlington men, Ordnance Artificer 4th Class James Clifford Oxley and Able Seaman Joseph Henry Hoggett.[12]

HMS Thunderbolt *returning from a patrol.* (Public Domain)

The crew of HMS Thunderbolt *with their Jolly Roger.* (Public Domain)

With the Battle of the Atlantic finally seeming to turn in the favour of the Allies the Germans introduced new torpedo technology in an attempt to redress the balance. On 20 September 1943 two convoys had come under repeated attack and the Flower-Class corvette HMS *Polyanthus* was called to render assistance. Two other escorts, HMS *Escapade* and HMS *Lagan* had both been badly damaged by torpedo attacks and the escort HMCS *St Croix* had been sunk. HMS *Polyanthus* chased off one U-Boat but, while preparing to rescue survivors from the sunken Canadian escort, was herself hit and sunk by an acoustic homing torpedo. There was only one survivor from the crew of eight-five, but this survivor was also killed when the ship which had picked him up, HMS *Itchen*, was sunk by a torpedo within days. Among the crew of HMS *Polyanthus* was Able Seaman Raymond Callaghan, a 20-year-old Darlington man.

CHAPTER 9

Darlington Soldiers

In Darlington 1940 opened with a tragedy in which a young soldier from the town lost his life. Driver Herbert Slater (18) had joined the Territorials in the spring of 1939 and was serving with the Royal Army Service Corps. His father testified that he was happy with his life as a soldier. He had returned on leave to his home at Swinburne Road. Driver Slater had gone missing overnight on New Year's Eve and his father had reported the matter to the police.

At the subsequent inquest the coroner heard from Reginald James Jackson, a Darlington furniture maker. Mr Jackson related how he and his friend, Mr Harvey Fletcher, had been walking along the southern bank of the River Tees near to Low Coniscliffe when they saw Driver Slater go down to the riverbank and begin testing the ice with his foot. A little later they saw the young soldier halfway across the river on the ice. Although he seemed confident, Mr Jackson believed be was taking a grave risk and went back to shout for him to return. Gunner Slater turned back but a few minutes later they heard the sound of breaking ice and a splash as he fell into the river when the ice gave way. The two men ran back to him and saw that he was attempting to support himself with his arms on the ice but that it kept breaking away. Mr Jackson ran to get a rope while his friend ran to get a plank so that they could attempt a rescue but when they got back there was no sign of the young soldier. The coroner thanked the two men for their efforts and told them that if they had attempted a rescue immediately then they would likely have lost their own lives.[1]

Many of the young men who found themselves serving in the forces had trouble coping with the stresses that such duty entailed, and for some the problems proved insurmountable and resulted in tragedy.

For one young Darlington soldier the stress and strain of serving far from home in an unfamiliar environment proved too much. 18-year-old Signalman James Walker Edwin of Darlington was serving in the Royal Corps of Signals in the south of England but on 6 April his body was found in Epping Forest. Signalman Edwin had shot himself in the head and a verdict of suicide while the balance of his mind was disturbed was returned.

Into Action

We have already seen how the Norwegian Campaign quickly turned into a disaster. One of the Army regiments to be engaged in Norway was 1 Green Howards (Yorkshire Regiment). After the initial landings and advances, the British troops were quickly forced to retreat and on 28 April, as they attempted to retreat through the Gudbrandsalen Valley, the Green Howards were engaged in what became known as the Battle of Otta. A large number of Darlington men served in the regiment which had proud historic links with the town. As the German 196th Infantry Division, supported by tanks and artillery advanced up the Gudbrand Valley they were engaged by two companies of the Green Howards ('C' and 'D'). Despite being poorly equipped the British managed to destroy three enemy tanks before being forced to retreat by artillery fire. As they retreated that night they were once again engaged but managed to fight the German forces off. During the fierce fighting on 28 April 1940 at least three Darlington soldiers from 1 Green Howards were killed in the fighting. The three men were: Private Sidney Pentland (21); Private William Charles Charlton; and Private Alfred Coad (21).[2]

With the unexpected swiftness of the German advances in France and the Low Countries a chaotic situation following the German blitzkrieg resulted as resistance collapsed and military units disintegrated. This culminated, for the BEF, in a disorderly retreat to Dunkirk.

The chaos of this retreat resulted in the deaths of a number of Darlington men. Fusilier John Joseph Bowen was a 30-year-old married man who had been in the Army for eight years and had seen service in Palestine and Egypt. After leaving the Army he had worked at Robert Stephenson and Hawthorns Ltd but had remained on the list of reserves and so was called up at the beginning of the war. In February he had been home on leave. Fusilier Bowen was killed on 24 May and is buried at the Wervicq (Sud) Communal Cemetery.[3]

At the beginning of June Mrs Margery Winifred Stephenson of Haughton-le-Skerne received news that her husband, Major William Stephenson, had been killed in action. Major Stephenson was well known in Darlington. Born in West Hartlepool, the major had lived in Haughton-le-Skerne since 1916 and was employed at the Stooperdale offices of the LNER, where he was assistant to the docks machinery engineer. In the First World War the major had served in the Royal Flying Corps. He was on the list of reserves and called up to serve with the Royal Engineers at the start of the war. Major Stephenson was 40 years of age and left behind his widow, an 11-year-old daughter and 4-year-old son. Like many who died in the chaotic fighting of this period, Major Stephenson has no known grave and is commemorated on the Dunkirk Memorial.

Another fatality of the fall of France and the Dunkirk evacuation was Corporal John Thomas Ferrier of 50th Divisional Signals, Royal Corps of Signals. On 28 May the 50th Divisional Signals received orders to withdraw to the coast, but on the following day Corporal Ferrier was killed in action. It appears, however, that he may have been wounded earlier and evacuated back to Britain because he is buried at Ramsgate Cemetery. Corporal Ferrier was a married man who lived at Vancouver Street and was well-known in the town. He had long been connected with the Boy Scouts Association in Darlington and had been scoutmaster of the 16th (Victoria Road Methodist) Troop for many years; in 1938 and 1939 he had been district scoutmaster.

In mid-June the town was thrilled to hear that two men from Darlington had been awarded the MM. These were the first medals earned by Darlington men during the war. Both were awarded to members of the Royal Corps of Signals. Both of the awards were given for actions which took place on 31 May during the Dunkirk evacuation. The first award went to Signaller G.E. Dean of Brinkburn Road. The second award was given to Corporal Luke Burnside (28) of North Road. Corporal Burnside's wife received the news of the award which was for showing great bravery in establishing and maintaining cabling from divisional headquarters to brigade during a thirty-six-hour period of heavy bombardment. Corporal Burnside had also shown courage and considerable initiative when tasked with laying telephone lines. By the time the award was announced, Corporal Burnside was back in Britain with his unit and, indeed, had recently been home on a short leave. Corporal Burnside had some renown as a singer in his hometown. He had been a leading tenor in the St Mark's Church choir and was a member of the Darlington Operatic Society.

The SS *Mohamed Ali El-Kebir* was an Egyptian-owned liner which had been used on Mediterranean routes before the war but she and her sister ship had been requisitioned at the start of the war and converted to troop ships. On 7 August 1940 she was in the Western Approaches bound for the Mediterranean with almost 700 soldiers from the Royal Engineers, Royal Pioneer Corps, Royal Artillery, the Intelligence Corps and a mixture of other units. At 9.40pm the *U-38* fired two torpedoes at the troop ship. One hit the vessel and she began to settle by the stern. An escorting destroyer, the HMS *Griffin*, chased off the submarine and then returned to pick up survivors. The troop ship launched eleven lifeboats and twenty rafts while HMS *Griffin* launched its two whalers. The sea was rough and some lifeboats and rafts were swamped.

Aboard the SS *Mohamed Ali El-Kebir* the ship's doctor, Stuart Liston, and a military medical officer remained, treating the injured so that they could be evacuated. As HMS *Griffin* picked up survivors she continued to drop depth charges to keep submarines away. Two hours after she had been hit, the troop ship sank. HMS *Griffin* remained in the area until the next morning and successfully rescued 766 survivors. Ninety-six lives were lost, eighty-two of them were soldiers who had been passengers, while the remaining casualties included nine Merchant Navy personnel, four Royal Navy and the ship's master, Captain John Thompson. The brave Captain Thompson had remained aboard until the last lifeboat was launched and was last been seen aboard a life-raft.[4]

One of the survivors from the SS *Mohamed Ali El-Fekir* was 20-year-old Darlington soldier, Driver R.W. Bowes of the Royal Corps of Signals. Driver Bowes, of Coniscliffe Road, related how he had jumped overboard and swum to a raft upon which he and three other men had floated throughout the night in rough conditions for six hours before they were picked up by HMS *Griffin*. The destroyer took the survivors to Greenock and, within days, Gunner Bowes was back in Darlington on survivor's leave. Prior to the war he had worked alongside his father on the staff of the Darlington Borough Treasurer's Department.

Many of the young men who found themselves serving in the forces had little experience and with road traffic increased as military units moved around the country there was an increase on the frequency of accidents, many of them unfortunately fatal, and a large number happening in the blackout. On the first day of October 1940 just such an accident claimed the life of a young Darlington soldier. Signalman Leonard Howard (23) of the Royal Corps of Signals was killed at Otley when his motorcycle was in collision with a lorry.[5]

With the numbers of Darlington casualties increasing sharply, it is somewhat surprising that it took until May 1942 for the town to decide to form its own branch of the Soldiers', Sailors' and Airmen's Families' Association. Major E.R. Hanby-Holmes of Barnard Castle explained at the inaugural meeting that the county was being reorganised and that, hopefully, this would mean that this would result in an increase in contributions.

On 23 October 1942, the Allies launched the Second Battle of El Alamein. Although the offensive was a resounding success and the beginning of the end of the North African campaign, seen by many as a turning point in the war (the church bells were rung for the first time since the beginning of the war to celebrate the victory), it came at the cost of over 13,500 Allied casualties (killed, wounded, captured or missing). Among those casualties on the first day of the twenty-day-long battle was 20-year-old Darlington lad, Private Derrick William Butler serving with 5th East Yorkshires. His body was never recovered and he is commemorated on the Alamein Memorial along with 11,869 others.

Many of the men taken prisoner by Japanese forces were ferried around various islands to undertake work details. The ships which were used to ferry them became known as 'hell-ships' due to the appalling conditions onboard. Among the victims of the Japanese 'hell-ships' was Darlington journalist Lance Corporal John Vincent McDonald (29). John, a married man, had joined the Royal Corps of Signals and was captured by the Japanese in early 1942, ending up in the Tandjon Priok Transit Camp on Java. Inspired by his journalistic instincts, Lance Corporal McDonald kept a diary of his time in camp. The diary featured a story of how some of the men would gather at the camp fence to watch the glorious sunsets over the neighbouring dock, dreaming of freedom and of family. Lance Corporal McDonald expressed the hope that every sunset brought him closer to freedom, but on 22 October he was among 1,100 prisoners loaded aboard the 'hell-ship' *Singapore Maru* to sail to Singapore, before sailing for Japan to work in the coal mines on Honshu. The rusted hulk was infested with rats and cockroaches and the prisoners, each allocated a small shelf, did not have enough room to either lie down or to sit up. The emaciated PoWs quickly fell victim to diseases and on 19 November, Lance Corporal John Vincent McDonald died of dysentery and exhaustion. On the next morning his body, wrapped in a weighted blanket, was slipped overboard, overseen by a padre who was himself almost too weak to stand. The former journalist's few possessions, including his diary, were collected by Captain Atholl Duncan, of the Argyll and Sutherland Highlanders. By the time the *Singapore Maru* arrived off Japan, some 106 of her passengers were dead and a further 260 were left aboard as they were too sick to move. Captain Duncan survived the war and, following his return home, sought out some of the relatives of those who had died. He had been so moved by the description of the sunsets in John McDonald's diary that he had copied it out in longhand and retained it.[6]

1943

For those serving in the harsh conditions of North Africa, disease could be just as deadly as the enemy and large numbers of men succumbed to various illnesses. On 16 February, Gunner Sopwith William Trevena (20) died in Algeria. Gunner Trevena was a member of the 59th Heavy Anti-Aircraft Regiment but it is unknown if the young Darlington Gunner died of wounds or illness.[7]

Many Darlington men served in the deserts of North Africa and one, Gunner G.H. Burden, found himself the centre of some local attention following the Battle of Sidi Nsir. The hamlet of Sidi Nsir became one of the focal points of the Germans' last offensive in Tunisia when it was attacked in force on 26 February. The Germans attacked with thirteen infantry battalions, 13,000 men, with supporting troops numbering 30,000 on the northern flank. The hamlet and railway station were quickly taken but 5 Hampshire Regiment, 172nd Field Regiment, RA, and 155 Battery, RA, were holding a position at a nearby farm. The men of the units were largely inexperienced and had no battle experience. For an entire day the British units held out against tanks, self-propelled guns, infantry and aircraft but suffered heavy casualties and by nightfall only one anti-tank gun and several machine guns were still operable. The final radio message received from the British position was 'Tanks are on us', and the position was at last overrun. The stand at Sidi Nsir had, however, bought valuable time for the defenders of Hunt's Gap further back, and allowed the organisation of a deep zone of defence there. The British forces at Sidi Nsir had amounted to nine officers and 121 other ranks, but only nine men reached British lines, seven of them wounded. One of these nine men was Gunner

Burden. Unfortunately, he was captured shortly thereafter and became a PoW. Burden had been a teacher at Darlington Grammar School and the University of London. His parents received the news of their son's capture at their home at Clifton Road.

While the majority of men who lost their lives in service during 1943 were aircrew there were numbers of Darlington men killed in the fighting in the Mediterranean. The Germans were in retreat in Tunisia but the village of Madjez-el-Bab had been on the front lines since December 1942 and there had been almost continuous fighting in the vicinity. On 2 March the village was again the scene of intense fighting as the Allies attempted the push to remove the remaining German presence from North Africa. On that day Lance Corporal Eric Snailham, a 27-year old married Darlington man was killed while serving with 16th Durham Light Infantry.[8]

Still others lost their lives in the fighting against the Japanese or in the appalling conditions of the Japanese prison and work camps. One of the latter was Gunner Ralph Joffre Dye. Gunner Dye had been a member of 7 Coast Regiment, Royal Artillery, stationed at Singapore when the Japanese invaded in 1942. It would seem that Gunner Dye (25) had been taken prisoner, but little more is known of him except for the fact that his parents back in Darlington were later informed that he had lost his life on 5 March 1943.[9]

The fighting in the deserts of North Africa had turned decisively in the Allies' favour but resistance remained fierce and many Darlington families knew that loved ones were facing great dangers in the desert. As the fighting in Tunisia reached a climax the Allies assaulted successive German defensive positions in March and April. On 25 March 1943 Private William Wilfred Johnson of 8th DLI was killed, aged 22. Private Johnson lived with his parents at Cockerton, Darlington, and is buried at Sfax War Cemetery.

The fighting to oust the Germans from North Africa claimed another Darlington victim on 6 April 1943 when 27-year-old Lieutenant John McGilvray of 5th Seaforth Highlanders was killed in action.

Lieutenant McGilvray was the eldest son of Charles and Margaret McGilvray. At the time of his death his parents were resident at Gallowsink Farm, Kirkintilloch, but by 1945 seem to have been living in Darlington. His bereaved mother placed commemorative pieces in several local newspapers throughout the wartime years and after.[10]

On 14 May 1943 the remaining German forces in Tunisia surrendered and the Allies immediately undertook preparations for the invasion of Sicily. The triumph in North Africa necessitated the shifting of many different Army units and a large number of convoys ferried men to new locations. On 16 June the SS *Yoma* left Tripoli bound for Alexandria. On board she had 134 officers and 994 other ranks from the British Army and 665 officers and men from the Free French Forces. Many of the British troops were Royal Engineers, including 994 Dock Operating Company and 1010 Dock Operating Company, who were to set up dock facilities at Alexandria in preparation for the invasion of Sicily. On the following morning, shortly after 7.30am and with many of the men below decks having breakfast, a German U-Boat fired two torpedoes at the ship. One, or possibly both, hit home and the *Yoma* quickly sank; 484 men were killed, 451 of them being military personnel. There were two Darlington men among the dead from the 994 Dock Operating Company. Lance Corporal Richard Quincey (27) and Lance Corporal Lancelot Nicholson Taylor (35) are both commemorated on the Brookwood 1939–1945 Memorial.[11]

The Allied invasion of Italy, which began on 3 September 1943, made rapid progress but there was fierce resistance from the German forces (the Italians had entered into an armistice and then re-joined the war on the side of the Allies) and the fighting grew gradually more bitter with heavy casualties being suffered. Many of the units in the thick of the action were those who had fought through the North African campaign which had so recently ended. On 19 September another Darlington soldier lost his life. Corporal Joseph Bland was a 33-year-old member of the 16th DLI.[12]

By October 1943 the Allied forces in Italy were facing the Germans' winter defensive line, codenamed 'Gustav'. The initial probing of this position demonstrated that it was a very secure defensive position and casualties were very heavy as the Allies tried to penetrate the position. On 1 October, 21-year-old Darlington soldier Trooper George Gustave Schott was killed in action while serving with the armoured cars of the 46th Regiment, Reconnaissance Corps, Royal Armoured Corps.[13]

On Remembrance Day 1943 another Darlington soldier lost his life in Italy. Private Robert William Todd was serving with the 7th Oxford and Bucks Light Infantry when he was killed. Like so many during the Italian campaign, the 21-year-old soldier's body was not recovered and he is commemorated on the Cassino Memorial. On the night of 10/11 November the battalion was ordered to aid the Guards in mounting an attack on Monte Camino. The attack met heavy resistance and at dawn on 11 November it became clear that the two forward companies on the right of the advance were in serious trouble, being surrounded on three sides by high ground. These companies were later forced to retreat under heavy fire and the attack failed with the Ox and Bucks suffering heavy casualties for practically no gain in territory whatsoever.

On 24 November the Allied forces that had fought their way north up Italy's Adriatic coast launched a crossing of the River Sangro, where defensive positions had been established. The crossing was a success and, after heavy fighting, the entire ridge above the river was secure by 30 November. On the first night of the crossing 37-year-old Private James Frederick Cade of the Royal Army Ordnance Corps was killed. Private Cade, a married Darlington man, was buried where he fell initially, but in May 1944 his body was moved to the Sangro River War Cemetery.

The fighting to take over the positions on the Sangro claimed another Darlington man on 30 November 1943 when 34-year-old Corporal George Teasdale of the Queen's Own Royal West Kent Regiment was killed. Corporal Teasdale was another married man and he also left behind a young son. Like Private Cade, he is buried at the Sangro River War Cemetery.

The fierce fighting in Italy claimed further Darlington lives in December 1943. Private William Milner was killed, aged 34, while serving with the 16th DLI, a battalion that had seen a great deal of action in North Africa and Italy. This courageous soldier was buried at the Cassino War Cemetery. Yet again, the death left bereft relatives in Darlington. Private Milner left behind his parents, William and Amelia, and a widow, Margaret. His family were obviously proud of the sacrifice made by Private Milner and had the following inscription placed upon his headstone: AND THUS HE WENT A NOBLE MAN ... TO SHIELD HIS HOME AND THOSE HE LOVED, A NOBLE SACRIFICE.

Although the Allied attack on the defensive positions at the Sangro River in Italy had been successful, fierce fighting continued on the area throughout the final month of 1943. On 28 December 32-year-old Corporal Norman Heron was killed while serving with the 1st Green Howards (Yorkshire Regiment). Corporal Heron was married to a Darlington woman and lies, along with several other men from Darlington, at the Sangro River War Cemetery.

1944

The people of Darlington awoke on the morning of 6 June 1944 to the heartening news that the D-Day landings were underway across the Channel. Although the vast majority of residents welcomed the news, a large number also suffered anxiety as they realised that loved ones would probably be involved in the invasion. At least four Darlington men died on 6 June as part of Operation Overlord. One such man was 28-year-old Lance Sergeant Robert Fenwick, serving with the 2nd East Yorks when he was killed in action. The battalion had landed on Queen Red Beach on Sword Beach and, under heavy fire, had pushed inland to assault two strongpoints (codenamed cod and sole) before eliminating the Daimler Battery and the village of St Aubin d'Arquenay, and spending the night in fields near Hermanville. By the end of the day, the battalion had lost sixty-five officers and men killed and 141 wounded. 25-year-old Sapper Charles Lockhart was serving with 1018 Port Operating Company, Royal Engineers; 21-year-old Private Henry Redding was serving with the 7th Green Howards and had landed with his battalion on Gold Beach in the first wave of the attack. By the end of the day the Green Howards had fought their way seven miles inland. 24-year-old Sapper Alan Oakley Walker was serving with 629 Field Squadron, Royal Engineers.[14]

1945

In early 1945 as German resistance crumbled towards the end of the war in Europe those Darlington folk who had loved ones still serving in the European Theatre had the added fear that their loved one might well be killed when the war was in its final weeks while others looked forward to the day they would return home. One Darlington soldier, however, played a role in the surrender of the Nazi forces in north-west Germany. On VE-Day the local press carried stories of how Sergeant J. Kerman of Dodds Street, Darlington, had been the first man to speak to the German officers who offered the surrender. Sergeant Kerman told how the battle was still raging and that he was on a reconnaissance mission close to Hamburg when he noticed two German officers walking towards them under a white flag. Together with a sergeant major of the Argylls, he drove up to speak to them and they told him they wished to speak to an officer.

CHAPTER 10

Darlington and Teesdale
Airmen and WAAFs

Two days after the HMS *Royal Oak* was sunk, German aircraft mounted an attack on naval vessels in the Firth of Forth. One of the units involved in defending the area was 607 Squadron. Among the airmen scrambled to the interception was Pilot Officer Henry Peter Dixon. Together with his section he dived down to protect HMS *Mohawk* which was under attack. The *Mohawk* gunners, however, fired upon the Gloster Gladiators and they were forced to withdraw. Pilot Officer Dixon was the second son of John and Elsie Dixon. The family lived at a house called 'Quarriston' in the pretty village of Heighington. Henry Peter Dixon, known to his friends and family as Peter, had a well-off upbringing as his father was a director of the Cleveland Bridge Company in Darlington. Peter had been educated at Cambridge University where he had studied engineering. He also joined the university air squadron and qualified as a pilot in 1936. Returning home to work at his father's firm, he joined 607 (Co. Durham) Squadron of the Auxiliary Air Force. Peter had spent several months in India during 1937–39 but re-joined his squadron in August 1939. In mid-November, 607 Squadron was dispatched to France as part of the Air Component of the British Expeditionary Force (BEF) and undertook a number of patrols in its aging Gladiators.

With the RAF expanding rapidly the training machine was, at times, overwhelmed and accidents became more common. The first Darlington airman to lose his life in 1940 was involved in such a training accident. Aircraftman 2nd Class (AC2) William Alfred Squires was 19 years old and a member of 9 Bombing and Gunnery School (BGS) based at RAF

Penrhos in Wales. One of the problems of expanding training so rapidly was that a wide variety of obsolete aircraft types were often used as trainers. On 6 February, AC2 Squires was detailed as the drogue operator in a Westland Wallace II (K8687) on a routine gunnery practice flight over the sea. The Wallace's engine cut out and the aircraft was ditched in the sea off Pwllheli but overturned. The pilot escaped from the aircraft but AC2 Squires was drowned. A subsequent inquiry revealed that the pilot had not been properly instructed in the aircraft's fuel system.[1]

Flying Officer Peter Dixon had a cheerful reunion at the end of February when he met up with his older brother John, a major serving in the Royal Artillery. Peter, who was still with 607 Squadron in France, had been promoted to Flying Officer on 5 January. Shortly afterwards, the squadron traded in its aging Gladiators for the far more impressive Hurricane.

With the successful Nazi invasion of Denmark and Norway the Wehrmacht were now in control of the two Scandinavian countries

A Westland Wallace II similar to that in which AC2 Squires lost his life. (Public Domain)

Above: *Pilots of 607 Squadron in France in 1940. Flying Officer Peter Dixon is in front of the window.* (Public Domain)

Left: *Flying Officer Peter Dixon.* (Public Domain)

and the pace of night bombing operations against targets in both countries, but especially Norway (with its wealth of natural resources and harbour facilities), intensified. On the night of 30 April/1 May operations were mounted against a number of Danish and Norwegian airfields. The raiding force consisted of fifty aircraft, thirty-five of which reported bombing their targets. However, the dubious value of these raids came at the cost of seven aircraft, four of which crashed on return to England. Among the latter was Hampden I (L4119) of 61 Squadron. The Hampden, from RAF Hemswell, Lincolnshire, crashed at 4.40am just six miles from Grantham after more than nine hours in the air. The Hampden would have been very low on fuel at the time and had ran into low cloud and poor weather and may have been damaged or suffering from mechanical problems. Whatever the cause, the aircraft flew into the ground and all four of the crew were killed. One of the wireless operator/air gunners killed in the crash was AC1 John Bell Greenall, known as Jack, a 22-year-old Darlington man. AC1 Greenall was an experienced airman having been in the RAF for two-and-a-half years. He had flown on a number of raids including those on the air base at Sylt. This was an island off the coast of northern Germany and was an important base housing, among other units, seaplanes.[2]

The Phoney War (largely referred to as the Bore War in Britain at the time) came to an abrupt and violent halt when the Nazis launched their attack on France and the Low Countries on 10 May. By dawn the next day the German forces had overrun the first lines of defence and the Allied armies were begging for aid from the RAF. Such was the growing desperation of the situation in France that 110 Squadron, based at RAF Wattisham, Ipswich, were used to bolster the RAF forces in that country. On the afternoon of 11 May, the RAF made an attack with twenty-three Bristol Blenheims on some vital bridges at Maastricht. Two of the Blenheims, both from 110 Squadron, failed to return and little damage was done to the bridges. Blenheim IV (N6208) took off from Wattisham at 2.50pm but was seen to crash on fire on the southern outskirts of Bethune. Two of the crew survived but were injured; the observer, Sergeant Arthur Colling (20) died later the same day from his injuries. Sergeant Colling was a Darlington man and was possibly the first Darlington member of aircrew to be killed in action in 1940.[3] He had been in the RAF for approximately eighteen months and had been home on leave the week before he was posted as missing. His parents were notified at their home at Cartmell Terrace, Darlington. Sergeant Colling was from a military family as both his father and grandfather had served with the Northumberland Fusiliers.

Among those who found themselves facing the German Blitzkrieg was Flying Officer Peter Dixon of 607 Squadron. Dixon flew throughout the first day of that offensive and shared a claim in the destruction of a Heinkel He111 bomber in the afternoon. Later in the evening he was awarded a victory over another He111 and one damaged. On the following afternoon Dixon was awarded with a share in another He111 and another damaged, but was forced to crash-land and make his way back to the squadron. His parents received a telegram informing them that he was missing because he did not return to the squadron until 12 May. On the afternoon of 15 May, Dixon claimed two HE111s destroyed. On 17 May Dixon flew his last sortie with 607 Squadron which, due to losses and casualties, was no longer combat-ready. During his brief time in action with 607 Squadron, he had flown fifteen sorties, claimed three aircraft destroyed, shared in the destruction of another two and a further two damaged.

Flying Officer Dixon had been returned to England for a few days' leave but he was ordered to report to 145 Squadron at RAF Tangmere, Chichester. The squadron was flying sweeps and patrols over Dunkirk and the evacuation area and regularly encountering the Luftwaffe. On the evening of 22 May he claimed two victories, but neither was officially confirmed. Dixon flew constant patrols for the next few days but was allowed two days' leave to recover from the constant strain of flying combat patrols. He spent the leave locally with another pilot from the squadron.

On 24 May 1940 the hurried training regime claimed the life of 23-year-old Sergeant Ernest Wigham, another Darlington airman native.[4] Late on the morning in question several Fairey Battle aircraft from 12 Operational Training Unit (OTU) took off to undertake navigational exercises. The pilots of the aircraft had been told to maintain radio silence but the weather conditions deteriorated with low cloud moving in. One of the Battles from the OTU crashed into Fire Beacon Hill near Sidmouth, killing all three crewmen. Twenty minutes later Battle I (K9481) crashed into the same hill, once again all three crew were killed.

Flying Officer Peter Dixon returned from leave on 28 May and was immediately thrust once again into combat covering the Dunkirk evacuation. On Saturday 1 June, 145 Squadron was ordered to patrol the Dunkirk area and they took off at 5.40am to make their way over the Channel. This patrol was uneventful with no enemy sighted, but the Luftwaffe succeeded in sinking three British destroyers (HMS *Basilisk*, HMS *Keith* and HMS *Skipjack*). 145 Squadron was back in the air at 11am with similar orders and on this occasion they sighted approximately seventy-five Messerschmitt Me109 and Me110 fighters. Although vastly outnumbered (there were only nine of them) they immediately dived down to attack. On this occasion Flying Officer Dixon was flying at the rear of the formation in the dangerous position known as 'a weaver'. One aircraft from 145 Squadron failed to return. Hurricane I (P22) with Flying Officer Peter Dixon was later confirmed as having been shot down by enemy fighters.

Troops waiting to be evacuated from Dunkirk watched the aerial fight above them and saw one aircraft come down on fire, followed by an airman whose parachute was on fire. The airman was pulled from the sea and taken to the dressing station on the Mole (a man-made jetty). One of those who witnessed the event was Major

John Dixon, who had no idea that the airman he had seen was his younger brother. Major Dixon returned to Britain the following day and was notified, along with his parents, that Peter was missing. For the Dixon family this was the beginning of an agonising period of waiting for news of Peter.

One of the most daunting of tasks facing RAF Coastal Command at this stage of the war was in trying to locate and intercept German shipping. On 27 June 1940 several Bristol Blenheim IVs of 235 Squadron took off from their base at Bircham Newton, tasked with patrolling the IIjsselmeer (a large closed off inland bay) in northern Holland. The Blenheims were intercepted by a large number of Messerschmitt Me109s and were shot down. Among the eleven fatalities from the twelve aircrew aboard the Blenheims was another Darlington airman: 28-year-old Sergeant Sidney Kendal Bartlett, observer aboard Blenheim IV (P6957), shot down into the North Sea off Holland at 3.30pm.[5]

Although the most visible aspect of the Battle of Britain were the fighter pilots and airmen of Fighter Command, RAF Bomber Command was also operating nightly to attack targets of military value. The most frequent targets during the period were enemy airfields and the German-held Channel ports, where it was thought invasion barges were being readied. On the night of 12/13 August, Bomber Command sent seventy-nine aircraft to attack various targets in France and Holland. Hampden I (P4379) was tasked with attacking Salzburgen but nothing more was heard from this aircraft, nor from another 61 Squadron aircraft which was sent to the same target. The observer was Flight Sergeant Wilfred Ward, the son of John and Harriet Ward of Darlington.[6]

Although many of those airmen who lost their lives in training were killed while in the final stages of their training, often at OTUs, others were killed earlier in the training process. Sergeant William Denys Hilton was a 21-year-old trainee pilot from Darlington and on 12 September 1940 he was based at 8 Flight Training School (FTS).

at RAF Montrose in Scotland. On the day in question he was flying solo in a Miles Master I (N7881) engaged upon a solo sortie for which he been briefed to practise map reading and steep turns. While two miles west of Laurencekirk, the Master stalled at approximately 300ft and entered a diving turn before crashing, killing Sergeant Hilton. He is buried at Darlington West Cemetery and his parents had the following inscription placed upon his headstone: HE SLEEPS IN GOD'S BEAUTIFUL GARDEN IN THE SUNSHINE OF PERFECT PEACE. A bird-bath dedicated to his memory was also erected next to his headstone.

As we have seen, not all casualties in the forces were a result of enemy action. Accidents continued to claim a large number of lives throughout the war. In October there was a particularly tragic accident. AC2 Herbert Sigsworth was posted to RAF Dumfries and was a part of 10 BGS when he sustained an accidental gunshot wound, he subsequently died in Dumfries Infirmary on 27 October 1940. Before joining the RAF, 31-year-old Sigsworth had worked at the grocery branch of the Darlington Co-operative Society at Dinsdale. He had been a keen swimmer and an active member of the Darlington Amateur Swimming Club and the Darlington water polo team. Herbert had married Isobel Robson of Bensham Road, Harrowgate Hill, Darlington, on 12 October, just fifteen days before his death in the unexplained accident. The body of the young airman was brought back home and he lies in Darlington West Cemetery.

In November, the father of Flying Officer Peter Dixon finally made some progress in the quest for the fate of his son. He traced and met with a Flying Officer Carswell, RNZAF, who had been shot down with 43 Squadron on the same day as his son. Carswell had seen Peter after he had been recovered from the sea and reported that Peter had been taken to the Café Jonval with severe burns to his face, hands and feet. The last Carswell had seen of him was when Peter was loaded into an ambulance to be taken to the casualty station on the Mole (a large landing jetty). On 26 November, more evidence was uncovered which revealed that Flying Officer Dixon had been taken from 10 Casualty Clearing Station (CCS) (on the Mole) and transferred to 12 CCS at Chateau Chapeau Rouge at Rosendael. This was due to an order from the commander of 10 CCS that only walking wounded could be evacuated aboard ship.

1941

With the RAF expanding rapidly it had become clear that the existing training system in Britain would probably not be able to cope with demand. The result was the Empire Air Training Scheme in which young men who had volunteered to train as air crew were posted to various locations in the Empire to complete their training. Recruits found themselves posted to Canada, Rhodesia, India and other far-flung places (later on some were even trained in America). The scheme was an overwhelming success, but one of the early requirements was the need for pilot instructors in the countries selected. As a result, a number of RAF pilots were posted abroad to act in this capacity. One of these men was Sergeant John Clydesdale Bell. Sergeant Bell was the son of a colliery official at Greenside Colliery in the west of Co. Durham but the family had moved to Ferryhill, Co. Durham, in 1938. John had served in the Merchant Navy but had enlisted in the RAF in 1936 and was married to a Darlington woman, Doris. On 13 March 1941 Sergeant Bell was killed in a mid-air collision.[7] The war brought more tragedy for the Bell family when John's younger brother, Flight Lieutenant Matthew William Bell (23), was killed on an operation to Lutzkendorf on 14/15 March 1945.[8]

Although the airmen of Bomber Command were faced with incredibly dangerous duties it was not only the airmen who faced danger. Those groundcrew who were charged with maintaining the aircraft upon which the lives of the crew depended also faced dangers, working at pace, on heavy machinery and often in darkness or hazardous conditions. On 9 May 1941, Corporal Arnold Delday Dearden (22), a Darlington man, lost his life while on active service with 207 Squadron at RAF Waddington. Corporal Dearden was a trained wireless operator and technician and had been in the RAF since 1936. His late father was the former curate of St Matthew's in Darlington. His mother received the telegram notifying her of her son's death at her home on Woodland Road. The unfortunate ground crewman is buried at Scarborough (Manor Road) Cemetery.

The losses amongst the men of the RAF continued apace. Many Darlington families had multiple sons serving in the RAF and other services and of those who were serving as aircrew the majority were employed as air gunners or wireless operators. The air gunners had a particularly dangerous role as they were often the first target for enemy fighters during an attack and the losses were horrendous. At the beginning of October 1941 Mr and Mrs Trevor Morris (Mr Morris was the manager of the Darlington branch of the Midland Bank) of Abbey Road received a telegram at their home which informed them that one of their sons, Sergeant John Ivor Morris, an air gunner in the RAF had been wounded in action and was in hospital in the south of England. Sergeant Morris (27) had a younger brother who was also serving in the RAF.

1942

As the newly installed commander of Bomber Command, Arthur Harris was keen to launch an operation which would both capture the imagination of the public and prove that his force was a viable attacking component of the war effort. He hit on the idea of using 1,000 bombers to raid a single target on one night and chose Cologne for the first such 1,000 raid. In order to get enough aircraft Harris had to use hundreds of training command aircraft in addition to his own full main front line strength. The raid was a success and Harris sought to reinforce the message.

Harris had kept his thousand-strong force together and sent 956 aircraft to Essen on 1/2 June. The force employed a very similar plan to that which had been used at Cologne (bombed instead of Hamburg due to poor weather over the initial target) with the exception that, given the constant industrial haze problems at Essen, the experienced raid leaders carried a higher proportion of flares than in the previous raid. Despite this and a fair weather forecast the target was obscured with a ground haze and bombing was therefore scattered, with Essen reporting only minor damage. Eleven other nearby towns were also hit, including Duisburg, Mulheim and Oberhausen. A total of thirty-one Bomber Command aircraft were lost on the raid along with three aircraft on intruder operations.

On this night there was a Darlington casualty. To scrape together enough aircraft the training command once again made a significant contribution to the raid. 12 OTU suffered just one casualty on the Essen raid. Wellington IC (X3203) had taken off from RAF Chipping Warden under the command of P/O M.N. Aicken, RNZAF, but was hit by flak while flying at 14,000 feet over the target. Four of the five crew survived but the observer, F/Sgt Arthur William Dormand, RAF, was killed. Dormand was aged 22 and the son of Arthur and Jane Dormand from Darlington.[9]

This second 1,000 raid took the life of at least one more Darlington airman when Lancaster I (R5844) of 106 Squadron failed to return to RAF Coningsby. The Lancaster had taken off at 12.45am with some very experienced crew aboard. Nothing further was heard, however, and the authorities later confirmed that all seven airmen had been killed. The mid-upper gunner was Sergeant Thomas Ernest Hodgson (28).[10]

June proved to be a bad month for Darlington airmen with at least three losing their lives in action. The next Darlington fatality was another mid-upper gunner. F/Sgt Charles Ronald Metcalfe was killed on 4 June during a raid on Bremen. This was a smaller raid consisting of 170 aircraft. The raid was successful but eleven bombers failed to return. F/Sgt Metcalfe was in the crew of F/Sgt J.W. Stell. The crew had taken off from RAF Middleton St George in Halifax II (R9457, MP-A) of 76 Squadron but were shot down by a night fighter over Holland with only two of the crew surviving to be taken prisoner.[11]

The final casualty of June was Sergeant Henry Edward Noble, a 26-year-old rear gunner with 37 Squadron. On the night of 24 June Sergeant Noble took off with the crew of Flight Lieutenant C.P.T. Helliwell from Landing Ground 09 which was a simple desert landing strip utilised by the bombers which were supporting the 8th Army; they were to make an attack on Benghazi. Wellington IC (DV643) failed to return and nothing further was heard from the crew. All six airmen are commemorated on the Alamein Memorial.

The parents of F/O Peter Dixon from Heighington had been desperately awaiting some news of the fate of their younger son since he had been reported missing following a fight with enemy fighters over Dunkirk on 1 June 1940. In July 1942 a witness to his death came forward and the location of his grave was located in Dunkirk Town Cemetery. In the meantime, Peter's father had been conducting extensive enquires to try to find out what had happened to his son. In July F/O Peter Dixon's father was informed that further information had now come to life which confirmed the fate and final hours of his son's life. Major P.H. Newman, RAMC, had recently escaped from custody and returned to England and had filled in the details. Major Newman had been stationed at 12 CCS and confirmed that Peter had been brought in suffering from severe burns after his parachute had caught fire. The Major revealed that Peter subsequently died from his burn injuries but asked that the family be assured that he was not in great pain, had been cheerful when brought in and had slipped into a coma a few hours before his death. Major Newman concluded his statement by stating that 'he was a grand chap'.[12]

On the night of 11/12 August Bomber Command dispatched 154 aircraft to make an attack on Mainz. The attack was successful but came at a substantial cost: 78 Squadron at Middleton St George suffered particularly badly, losing four Halifaxes on the raid. Halifax II (W1061) had taken off at 9.37pm with W/O2 W.E. Lunan, RCAF, at the controls. Over the target the Halifax was coned by searchlights and badly damaged by flak. Both of the port engines were destroyed and several of the crew were wounded. As the bomber wallowed along it was attacked by a night fighter and crashed just east of Antwerpen. Two of the seven-man crew were killed, one evaded capture and the remaining four were taken prisoner. The fatalities were the pilot and the navigator. The navigator, Sergeant Francis Alfred Scotland, was a 36-year-old Darlington man.[13]

With British and Allied shipping being attacked by U-Boats in the Bay of Biscay and the Southern Atlantic, RAF Coastal Command asked for reinforcements. Bomber Command responded by detaching some crews from 10 OTU to St Eval to make anti-submarine patrols. The crews were made up of a mixture of students and instructors and the work was exceptionally dangerous as the old Armstrong-Whitworth Whitleys which they were flying were easy prey to fighter aircraft and technical malfunction. On 22 August, for example, the detachment lost two aircraft and crew. The first crew were safely picked up by a Spanish fishing boat, but the second was lost without trace and all six men were subsequently commemorated on the Runnymede Memorial. Pilot Officer C. Neve and his crew were lost in Whitley V (Z9294) and the crew included two men from Co. Durham. One of these men, rear gunner Sergeant Clifford Dodds, was 20 years old and from Darlington.

The heavy casualties among Darlington airmen continued into September. On 4/5 September Bomber Command sent 251 aircraft to Bremen and twelve failed to return. Lancaster I (R5755, EM-N) was piloted by Pilot Officer R.G. Rowlands, RAAF, and was shot down over the Ijsselmeer by a night fighter, killing all aboard. The mid-upper gunner was Darlington man, Sergeant John Wilfrid Atkinson who, at 31-years-old, was older than most aircrew. Darlington airmen were not being lost solely in attacks on Germany; in the Far East the campaign against Japanese forces continued. On 9 September 1942 Lockheed Hudson IV (AE523, T) was shot down by Japanese fighters while attacking the port of Akyab. One of the crew lost was Darlington man Pilot Officer George Oliver Maughan (22).

Many Darlington men had, as we have seen, joined the RAF, but a number of women from the town had also decided to enlist in the service and serve as WAAFs. On 28 September, Leading Aircraftwoman Eileen Dawson became the first Darlington WAAF to die on active service when she passed away in hospital at Bedford. The 20-year-old had worked in the offices of Robert Stephenson and Hawthorns Ltd and then the LNER offices at Bank Top before deciding to enlist. LAC Dawson had been due to be promoted to corporal just days after her death, which appears to have been from natural causes. On Saturday 3 October the funeral of LAC Dawson took place in her hometown. Several members of her unit attended along with her mother, family and friends. A service was held at St Mark's Church where Eileen had been a member of the bible class and the Girls' Friendly Society. There is some confusion online over the death of LAC Dawson as some sites state that she was killed in the crash of an Oxford aircraft in 1943. This seems to have originated from the fact that the CWGC originally listed her death with this incorrect year. LAC Dawson is buried at Darlington North Cemetery.

Those men who found themselves on the front-line of Bomber Command's war against Germany needed to maintain their efficiency if they were to have a hope of survival and training was constantly undertaken, especially by the less experienced aircrew. The full-moon periods when operations were generally severely curtailed provided the opportunities for such practice. On the afternoon of 10 October 1942, however, such a training exercise resulted in the death of a Darlington airman and his crew from 150 Squadron. The crew of Sergeant W.H. Allworth had taken off to undertake a training operation but as they approached the runway at RAF Elsham Wolds in gusty conditions the pilot lost control and the Wellington III (BK311) crashed at 3.21pm and caught fire. Five of the six-man crew were killed instantly, while the pilot died of his injuries soon afterwards. Sergeant

Norman Desmond Green (21) of Darlington was a wireless operator/air gunner in the Wellington. The body of Sergeant Green was taken home for burial at Darlington West Cemetery.

Just like in operations over Europe and Britain, those airmen who found themselves posted to the Western Desert also found that the weather conditions could prove just as deadly as the enemy. On 16 October a sandstorm claimed the life of another Darlington airman. Flight Sergeant John Leonard Rayner (24) was a member of the Western Desert Communications Unit and was flying in a Westland Lysander when he ran into a severe sandstorm. Flight Sergeant Rayner attempted to make an emergency landing in the desert but was killed when his plane crashed. Flight Sergeant Rayner was a former student at Darlington Grammar School. Like many who were lost in the desert war the body was never recovered and F/Sgt Rayner is commemorated on the Alamein Memorial.

The rather ramshackle aerial night defences of Britain had improved dramatically by 1942. The role of flying night fighters was a highly dangerous one and was fraught with risk even without enemy action. On the night of 5 November a flying accident claimed the life of another Darlington pilot when Beaufighter NF1 (V8272) of 141 Squadron, based at RAF Ford, crashed into a hill near to the village of Duncton, eight miles from Chichester. The pilot was Sergeant Kenneth Milburn (22) from The Leas, Harrowgate Hill, Darlington. Sergeant Milburn was well known in the town. He had been educated at Albert Road School and for some time had been involved with the local boy scout association, being assistant scoutmaster of the St Mark's Troop. Both Sergeant Milburn and his navigator/wireless (radar) operator, Sergeant John Robert Reginald Allison of Bishop Auckland, were killed in the crash. Sergeant Milburn had experienced a lucky escape in training when he had been training at 54 OTU and had crashed a Bristol Blenheim at RAF Church Fenton. Sgt Milburn lies in Darlington North Cemetery.

A flying accident on 18 December 1942 claimed the life of Flight Sergeant Thomas Raymond Furness, a 21-year-old Darlington-born member of 205 Squadron of South East Asia Air Command. Flight Sergeant Furness was part of the crew of Consolidated Catalina (AJ156, M) which crashed during a night-time take-off at Pamazani in the Comoros Islands.

1943

The year opened fairly quietly for the airmen of Bomber Command with the commanding officer, Arthur Harris, marshalling his forces in preparation for launching his main offensive later in the year. This did not mean, however, that the activities of the command ceased altogether. Pressure had to be maintained and so several smaller-scale raids took place in the first months of the war.

Bomber Harris had sent a small force of 148 aircraft to Hamburg on 30/31 January, but he followed this up with a larger raid consisting of 263 aircraft on 3/4 February. Harris had been saving his strength and this was the first raid to involve more than 200 aircraft in more than a fortnight. Among the force were sixty-six Short Stirlings drawn from 3 Group (based in East Anglia). The attack was a failure. Severe weather and icing caused many aircraft to turn back over the North Sea while sixteen bombers were lost, largely to enemy night fighters. Among these losses were eight Stirlings. At RAF Chedburgh, 214 Squadron lost two of its aircraft on this night, including that of one of its flight commanders. Stirling I (R9282, BU-Q) took off under the control of S/Ldr W. Clarke but was shot down by a night fighter south-west of Utrecht. Four of the crew were able to bale out and became PoW's but the remaining three were killed when the Stirling crashed. The navigator aboard the Stirling was Sgt George Eric Johnson, a 21-year old from Darlington.[14]

As we have seen, many Darlington men were enticed to join the RAF, many seeing the service as the most glamorous of the services. Although many undoubtedly dreamed of flying Spitfires with Fighter Command, the truth was that the vast majority would not be trained as pilots and would instead be trained in the other aircrew trades such as navigator, bomb-aimer, wireless operator or air gunner. In 1943 the majority of recruits to RAF aircrew would find themselves destined for Bomber Command.

The lengthy training process which was necessary to train raw recruits to crew the new advanced heavy bombers was an arduous one and was very dangerous. Many young men lost their lives in training accidents before they even got near to an operational squadron. Many of these accidents happened while crews were at the OTU stage of their training and were flying as crews for the first time.

On the morning of 11 March the experienced F/Lt P.S. Marriott, DFM, took off at the controls of Wellington III (X3874) of 15 OTU, based at RAF Harwell. The experienced tutor pilot was flying with an inexperienced crew and was instructing them on dual engine aircraft, familiarisation with the Wellington, and single-engine flying procedures. During the flight the port engine failed and the Wellington dived and crashed at 11:15 am beside Didcot. The fatal crash clamed the life of yet another embryo Darlington airman. Sgt John Edward Siddell was 26-years-old and yet another married man who had volunteered for aircrew service. Sgt Siddell left behind his parents and his widow and young daughter at Cockerton, Darlington.[15]

Attempting to protect the routes over the southern Atlantic proved to be problematic and often dangerous. 95 Squadron, with its Sunderland flying boats, fought a lonely battle over this part of the ocean. In March it had moved to Bathurst in Gambia. By this stage of the war the greatest threat to the crews of 95 Squadron came not from enemy action but from engine failures, which resulted in seven Sunderlands having to ditch at sea, several with the total loss of their crews. Only two of the aircraft were recovered. One of the other duties performed by the squadron was that of search and rescue. On 31 March 1943 a Sunderland from the squadron was tasked with searching for and, if possible, picking up survivors from the SS *Celtic Star*. HMS *Wastmaster* was on scene and was coordinating the rescue. The Sunderland (W6063, W) was approaching the scene but flew too low and hit a large wave before crashing into the sea. Three of the crew, along with the crew of the stricken merchant vessel, were picked up by HMS *Wastmaster*, but six of the Sunderland crew were killed and their bodies were not recovered. Among them was Sergeant George William Graham, a 31-year-old married man from Darlington.[16]

Even when an aircraft was not shot down there could still be casualties among the crew when it returned. On the night of 3/4 April, Bomber Command sent 348 aircraft to bomb the vital Ruhr target of Essen. The raid proved to be accurate and considerable damage was done, but twenty-one aircraft failed to return. One which did return was the 102 Squadron Halifax II (JB867), but the crew had experienced both extreme danger and tragedy. Over the target the Halifax, piloted by Squadron Leader John Everard Hadfield Marshall, DFC, RAF, had been coned by searchlights and Squadron Leader Marshall had been forced to take extreme evasive action which resulted in the aircraft being flown down to just 5,000ft. The bomber was hit multiple times by flak and the rear gunner, Flying Officer Thomas McLoughlin, was severely wounded. Despite the efforts of the crew, Flying Officer McLoughlin died of his wounds shortly afterwards. The damaged Halifax was piloted back to Britain but was so badly damaged that Squadron Leader Marshall put it down at an alternative airfield, possibly Breighton or Holme-on-Spalding-Moor. Flying Officer McLoughlin was 29 years of age, a native of Darlington where his parents, Thomas and Maud, still lived; he is buried in the town's West Cemetery.[17]

On 16/17 April, the main force from Bomber Command was sent to bomb the Skoda armaments factory at Pilsen in Czechoslovakia. A diversionary force from the command, consisting of 271 older aircraft, made an attack on the German city of Mannheim. The attack on Mannheim was a success, but came at the expense of eighteen aircraft from the attacking force. 166 Squadron at RAF Kirmington, Lincs, was still struggling along with its old Wellingtons and the squadron lost one aircraft that night when Wellington X (HE862) failed to return.

The Wellington had not, however, fallen victim to enemy action. It had developed engine trouble and had been forced to ditch in the Somme Estuary. The impact of the ditching was heavy and two of the crew did not survive. One of the victims was the pilot, Flying Officer Selwyn Jaques Lupton, a 22-year-old from Darlington. Flying Officer Lupton had been a good student before the war and had attained a 1st Class Honours Degree in English at Leeds University.[18]

Towards the end of April 1943 the local press announced that a Darlington navigator, though born at Shildon, serving with the RAF had been awarded the DFC for his actions while fighting in North Africa. F/O William Taylor Story's (33) citation mentioned his actions during daylight sorties, including four attacks on Benghazi and two on Tobruk. During one of the attacks on Benghazi the formation of bombers was attacked by enemy fighters and over the target F/O Story's aircraft was damaged by heavy and accurate anti-aircraft fire. Despite this the aircraft bombed the primary target successfully and it was F/O Story's accurate navigation which allowed his captain to nurse the crippled bomber back to base.

Training accidents continued to take their toll of Darlington airmen throughout the year as the training units attempted to get increasing numbers of crews ready for the now heightened pace of operations. At 1:44 am on 2 May the trainee crew of Sgt J.R. Richmond took off from RAF Westcott for a night practice flight to the ranges at Warpsgrove. An hour into the flight, however, control was, for unknown reasons, lost and the Wellington IC (Z8806) crashed to the ground seven miles from Oxford with total loss of life. It was subsequently reported that the pilot was flying solely on instruments at the time of the crash. The wireless operator on the flight was Darlington airman Sgt Thomas Nathaniel Harker (21).[19]

On 3/4 May Bomber Command sent 596 aircraft in a maximum effort raid on the city of Dortmund. This was the largest non-1,000 bomber raid of the war so far and demonstrated the growing strength of the Command. Severe damage was caused in Dortmund but thirty-one aircraft were lost. It was policy in Bomber Command for a newly arrived pilot to undertake a trip with an experienced crew before he flew on operations with his own crew. The policy was disliked by the experienced crews who often believed that taking a stranger, known as a 'second-dickie', could result in bad luck. On this night the experienced crew of Flight Lieutenant W.L. Turner, RCAF, from 218 Squadron had just such a passenger. Taking off in Stirling III (BF505, HA-Z) the crew set course for the target. Nothing more was heard and subsequent information revealed that the Stirling had been shot down by a night fighter over Holland shortly after 1am. Of the eight men aboard, three were able to bale out and survived as PoWs. The second-dickie pilot was not one of them. Sergeant Frank Norman Robinson was a 21-year-old from Darlington. His parents, Frederick and Annie, received the news of their son's death at their home in the town.

Although the now-obsolete Bristol Blenheim had been phased out of service over Europe, the type continued to operate with the RAF in other theatres. 11 Squadron was equipped with Blenheims and flew over the Burmese front. On 21 May Blenheim IV (Z7619) took off from Feni, Bangladesh, on a radar calibration flight. The Blenheim landed at Chittagong before taking off once more. Later, information came through that the bomber had been shot down by Japanese Zero fighters off Mickhall Island. A search party from Ramu was sent out and recovered the wreckage and the bodies of the five crew. The navigator in the crew was P/O Charles Pigdon, a 33-year old married man from Darlington. P/O Pigdon was buried at Chittagong War Cemetery and his mother and widow had a poignant inscription placed upon his headstone. It reads: EACH SUNSET BRINGS US ONE DAY NEARER. SADLY MISSED BY LOVING MOTHER & DEAR WIFE.

The recent RAF casualties from the town and the growing press attention that was being paid to Bomber Command undoubtedly brought the service to the forefront of many minds in the town and aided the Wings for Victory campaign. On 30 May yet another Darlington airman lost his life when the Wellington VIII (HX526) of 38 Squadron crashed on take-off from Misurata West, Libya. The wireless operator/air gunner aboard the Wellington was Sgt Leslie Hugh Butler, a 30-year old native of Darlington who left behind his parents, Bertram and Mary, and his widow, Daisy, in his hometown.[20]

On the night of 11/12 June a massive raid on Dusseldorf was undertaken by 783 aircraft from Bomber Command. Extensive damage was caused but 38 bombers were lost in the raid. It was a bad night for 12 Squadron at RAF Wickenby, Lincolnshire, which lost no less than five of its Lancasters along with thirty-two aircrew from the thirty-five men aboard. Lancaster I (ED357, PH-S) took off at 10:40 pm with Sgt Daniel McNicol Thomson, RAAF, at the controls. It is believed that the Lancaster was shot down by a night fighter over the Ijsselmeer shortly after 11 pm on its outward journey. Five of the seven crew were killed when the bomber crashed. The navigator was another Darlington man, Sgt Kenneth Bowes was a 23-year old married man. His body was never recovered and he is commemorated on the Runnymede Memorial.[21]

Bomber Command continued its campaign against the Ruhr on 28/29 June when a large-scale attack involving 608 aircraft was made on Cologne. Despite an inauspicious weather forecast this proved to be the most successful raid of the Battle of the Ruhr, although twenty-five aircraft were lost. Among them was Halifax V (DK137, NP-R) of 76 Squadron. The bomber had taken off from Holme-on-Spalding-Moor under the command of Sergeant G.C. Parritt, RAF. At 1.55am the Halifax was shot down by a night fighter over Liege, killing all seven of the crew. The flight engineer, 21-year-old Sergeant John Lawrence Burnside, was yet another young Darlington airman.[22]

With the Allies having successfully forced the Germans to abandon North Africa attention turned towards the invasion of southern Europe. The first step was Operation Husky, the invasion of Sicily, which began on 9 July. Before the invasion the RAF undertook preparatory bombing of several sites on Sicily. On the night of 5/6 July the Wellington bomber crews of 40 Squadron at Hani West were briefed to attack the airfield at Gerbini. Wellington X (HE793, Y) was to the north of the target area when it was attacked and shot down in flames. The entire five-man crew was killed when the Wellington crashed. The pilot was Sgt Walter Dench, a 22-years-old married man from Darlington.[23]

428 Squadron suffered its first casualty when one of its most experienced captains failed to return from Gelsenkirchen on 9/10 July. Halifax V (DK229, NA-W) and the crew of S/Ldr F.H. Bowden, DFC and Bar, failed to return. S/Ldr Bowden was one of the squadron's flight commanders and was nearing the end of his second operational tour. The Halifax was hit by flak in the vicinity of Cologne and S/Ldr Bowden ordered the crew to abandon while he held the aircraft steady. All of the crew managed to bale out but S/Ldr Bowden paid the price that many bomber pilots paid in remaining at his post until his crew had baled out of the aircraft and was killed.

On the night of 13/14 July several aircraft from the RAF bomber squadrons based in North Africa were tasked with bombing marshalling yards in the Sicilian city of Messina. Three aircraft, all Wellingtons, failed to return. One of these casualties was Wellington X (HE850, N) of 142 Squadron. The bomb-aimer in the six-man crew was F/O Nelson Avery, from Darlington. F/O Avery was an experienced airman and had previously been mentioned in dispatches.[24]

Although the Battle of the Ruhr was raging, Harris could not afford to send his force to the same target every night. Such tactics would have resulted in catastrophic casualties as the Germans would have been able to concentrate their defences around the Ruhr. There were also other demands placed upon Harris and he had to help keep up the pressure on Italy with raids to Italian targets. On the night of 12/13 July the crews of 295 Lancasters from 1, 5, and 8 Groups were briefed for an attack on Turin. Attacks on the more lightly defended Italian targets were generally less deadly than those on German targets, the crews painted ice-cream cones on their aircraft to symbolise these operations rather than bombs, but the long flight, much of it over occupied France, could still prove deadly and a steady stream of casualties came from these Italian operations. On this night, thirteen Lancasters failed to return, but overall the raid appears to have been a success. Among the casualties on this night was one of the 'stars' of Bomber Command, Wing Commander John Nettleton who had already won the VC for leading a low-level daylight raid on the German city of Augsburg in April. Wing Commander Nettleton, VC, was the commanding officer of 44 Squadron; he and his crew were all killed when their Lancaster was shot down by a night fighter. 156 Squadron of the Pathfinders lost one aircraft on this night; Lancaster III (ED919) had taken off from RAF Warboys, Cambs, at 10.48pm with Pilot Officer J.J. Hewerdine, RAAF, at the controls. Nothing more was heard of the aircraft, and the crew were subsequently posted missing believed killed. The bomb-aimer, Sergeant John Alan Walker (26), was yet another Darlington airman to lose his life. Like so many of the airmen of Bomber Command who lost their lives the body of Sgt Walker was never recovered and he is commemorated on the Runnymede Memorial.

There is some mystery surrounding the death of Sgt Robert Terry, a 35-years-old married man from Darlington. It is known that he lost his life on 10 August and was an air gunner. He is commemorated on the Runnymede Memorial. The roll of honour at St John the Baptist in the Co Durham village of Egglescliffe (where Sergeant Terry and his wife lived) states that Sergeant Terry lost his life on a bombing raid over Germany, but this appears unlikely as he is not listed as a casualty of the raid that was mounted that night. Instead, it seems likely that Sergeant Terry was one of the crew of a 3 OTU Wellington VIII (HX512) which went missing over the Irish Sea on an anti-submarine exercise.

The night of 31 August/1 September saw Arthur Harris send his force to attack the German capital once more. Bomber Command used 622 aircraft on this raid, including 106 of the now largely obsolescent Stirlings. The low-flying Stirlings were more at risk of enemy attack than the other bombers but their dangers also included becoming victim to the bombs of higher flying bombers above them. For 75 (New Zealand) Squadron at RAF Mepal the night was disastrous and ended with the loss of five of its bombers and their crews. Most of these bombers fell victim to enemy action but Stirling III (EH905, AA-R), piloted by P/O G.V. Helm, RNZAF, was hit by bombs over the target and crashed near Potsdam, killing five of the crew, although the two air gunners in the rear were able to bale out. The wireless operator/ air gunner in the Helm crew was Sgt Arthur John Bishop (22), RAF, a married man from Darlington.[25]

The RAF's campaign against Nazi Germany continued on several fronts and the action over the Italian front continued to cause casualties among Darlington men. 23 Squadron was a night fighter squadron base at RAF Luqa on Malta and was tasked with flying intruder operations over Sicily, Italy and Tunisia. At the beginning of September a detachment from the squadron was based at Sigonella on Sicily. On the night of 4/5 September the squadron was flying night disruption flights over Italy and upon return to Sigonella, one of the squadron's Mosquitoes crashed on landing, killing Sergeant Leslie Green, a 22-year-old native of Darlington.

Many of the more distant targets in Germany required the long winter nights for the aircraft of Bomber Command to operate against them. On the night of 2/3 October 1943, 294 Lancasters and two B-17s were sent to bomb the city of Munich. Despite there being clear conditions over the target, the marking was scattered and the bombing hit the south and south-eastern parts of the city. Lancasters from 5 Group, however, were practising a time-and-distance bombing method (requiring straight and level flight for a considerable period on the run up to the target), which was being put forward by their group commander. On this night the method failed and bombing from many of these aircraft fell some fifteen miles back along the approach route to the target. Of the eight Lancasters lost on this night, six came from 5 Group, and 207 Squadron at RAF Langar lost one aircraft that night. Lancaster III (DV-184, EM-O) took-off at 6.27pm but crashed almost immediately (apparently the pitot head cover had been left in place meaning that no air speed could be determined), killing all seven men of the crew. So violent was the crash that only three of the bodies could be identified. One of those which could not was that of the flight engineer, Sergeant Robert Mitchell Appleton, RAF. Sergeant Appleton was a 23-year-old Darlington man.[26]

We have already seen how many men lost their lives in the Japanese hell-ships but on 29 November 1943 there was a particularly tragic incident. The US submarine the USS *Bonefish* torpedoed what it believed to be a Japanese merchant vessel off Kangean Island. The SS *Suez Maru* was a hell-ship which was carrying 547 sick PoWs and over 100 wounded Japanese soldiers. Approximately half of the PoWs drowned when the ship sank but approximately 200 managed to jump into the water. Four hours later a Japanese minesweeper arrived on the scene. The Japanese captain picked up the Japanese and Korean survivors but then ordered that all of the PoWs in the water should be shot. Amongst those who lost their lives in the SS *Suez Maru* atrocity were two Darlington men. LAC Robert William Nicholson was 23-years of age and LAC Joseph Batty Alderson was 24-years-old and had served with 220 Squadron when he was taken prisoner. Both men are commemorated on the Singapore Memorial.

With Bomber Command's Battle of Berlin in full swing the losses and raids increased in tempo and severity. On 2/3 December 458 bombers were sent to attack Berlin once more. Taking a direct route to the German capital proved costly as enemy night fighters infiltrated the bomber stream. A total of 40 bombers failed to return from the raid and the bombing was scattered by weather conditions. One Lancaster from 630 Squadron failed to return to RAF East Kirby. Lancaster III (ED777, LE-Q) was reported to have crashed at Gross Schulzendorf, killing all seven crew, whose average age was just 22. The navigator was Flight Sergeant Richard Hooton Banks, RAF. Sergeant Banks was a 25-year-old from Darlington and had attained a 1st Class Diploma in Agriculture from Wye College, London University.[27]

With the Battle of Berlin continuing at ever greater cost, Harris once again sent his Command to the German capital on 16/17 December.

On this occasion an all-Lancaster main force of 483 aircraft was dispatched along with ten Mosquitoes. The raid was reasonably accurate but the straight-in course to Berlin allowed night fighters to engage the bomber stream and twenty-five Lancasters were lost. On returning to Britain the bombers found poor weather conditions and a further twenty-nine bombers were lost as they tried to find somewhere to land. On return, one aircraft from 57 Squadron was heard on wireless stating that it was being forced to ditch in the North Sea. A search was mounted but only one crewman was recovered alive from the sea. The Lancaster III (JB373, DX-N) was being flown by Sergeant John Walter Hinde, RAF, a 21-year-old from Darlington. The body of Sergeant Hinde and five of his crew were never recovered and the airmen are commemorated on the Runnymede Memorial.[28]

A second airman with strong Darlington connections lost his life on this raid. Flight Lieutenant Arthur Walker was a 31-year-old navigator with 12 Squadron. A native of Whitehaven in Cumbria, he had married a Darlington woman, and was part of the crew of Flight Sergeant H.R.H. Ross, RAAF. Taking off from RAF Wickenby at 4.14pm the Lancaster successfully attacked the target, but on return to Britain the bomber crashed at 11.45pm when some nine miles west-south-west of Louth in Lincolnshire. Six of the crew were killed instantly in the crash while the rear gunner, Sergeant R.A. Whitley, RAF, was severely injured and died shortly afterwards in Louth Hospital.[29]

As the year ended Bomber Command continued its main offensive against Germany but Harris realised that he had to send raids to other targets too. On the night of 20/21 December 650 aircraft were dispatched on a raid to Frankfurt. With casualties rapidly mounting during this Battle of Berlin period, the decision was made to send a force of forty-four Lancasters and ten Mosquitoes to make a diversionary attack on Mannheim in an effort to draw away the enemy night fighters. The German controllers tracked the bomber stream from an early stage and the distraction failed. There were a large number of combats with enemy night fighters recorded on the route into the target and losses were heavy with forty-one aircraft failing to return. The bombing was disappointing as the Pathfinder marking plan was disrupted by the presence of unexpected cloud cover. Damage in the city, however, was still substantial.

While a newer Halifax bomber, the Mk III, was now beginning to reach the squadrons the vast majority of Halifax squadrons based in Co Durham and North Yorkshire with 4 and 6 Groups were still having to make do with the now obsolescent older Halifaxes. On this night some 257 had been part of the force and 27 of them failed to return, some 10.5 per cent. 78 Squadron based at RAF Breighton lost five of its Halifaxes on this night. Amongst them was Halifax II (LM330, EY-O) piloted by F/Sgt A. Molloy, RAAF. Bomber Command was a proudly multi-national force with many bomber crews consisting of men of several nationalities. The crew of F/Sgt Molloy was, however, unusual in that it consisted of men from four air forces, representing Australia, Canada, New Zealand and the UK.[30] The bomber had taken off at 4:22 pm and had bombed successfully but on returning to base and awaiting permission to land the aircraft stalled and crashed near the village of Howden, just 4 miles from Breighton, shortly after midnight. The Halifax burst into flames on impact and the entire crew was killed. The flight engineer was Sgt Aubrey Denys Meynell, RAF. Sgt Meynell was a 21-years-old native of Darlington and his parents had their son buried in his hometown at Darlington West Cemetery.

By the summer of 1943 the U-Boats prowling the Bay of Biscay were taking a steady toll of Allied shipping. RAF Coastal Command made repeated attempts to sink these U-Boats but had suffered casualties due to enemy aerial attack. In August, three squadrons of Coastal Command Bristol Beaufighters, together with Mosquito fighter bombers from 10 Group of Fighter Command, were sent to Cornwall to provide fighter cover for the anti-submarine flights. One of these Coastal Command squadrons was 143 Squadron. On Christmas Eve the squadron was carrying out a patrol over the Bay of Biscay. The commander of the squadron, Squadron Leader William Storey Moore, and his wireless (radar) operator/navigator, Flying Officer Philip Heslop Froment, were in Beaufighter XI (JM160) when they sighted a German Heinkel He177 long-range heavy bomber. The crew made to attack the German aircraft but their Beaufighter, for unknown reasons, broke up in mid-air and both men were killed. Flying Officer Froment was a 20-year-old from Darlington. He and his pilot are commemorated on the Runnymede Memorial.[31]

1944

Amongst the squadrons which were part of 6 (RCAF) Group, Bomber Command, was 431 (Iroquois) (RCAF) Squadron. Although nominally a RCAF squadron there were airmen from various nationalities on the squadron. The Commonwealth air forces had not previously trained aircrew to act as flight engineers (the position had only come about with the use of the four-engine bombers) and many of the flight engineers on the Canadian squadrons were British. On the night of 20/21 January the Command had continued its campaign against Berlin but on the next night the tired aircrew were briefed once more for a long flight into Germany. The target on the night of 21/22 January was Magdeburg. 648 aircraft were sent on the attack, the first major one to this target. German night fighters infiltrated the bomber stream early and there were heavy casualties. Some 57 aircraft failed to return from the Magdeburg raid. 431 Squadron lost only one bomber on the raid. Halifax V (LK680, SE-R) had taken off from RAF Croft at 8:20 pm with F/Sgt H. Krentz, RCAF, at the controls. The Halifax was hit by flak and exploded over the River Weser near Bremerhaven. F/Sgt Krentz was blown out of the aircraft and survived to be taken prisoner, but the remaining six men of his crew were killed. The flight engineer in the crew was Sgt Clive Gilroy, a 19-years-old from Pierremont, Darlington. His parents had the following placed on his headstone: OF DARLINGTON, DURHAM. IN GOD'S SAFE KEEPING.[32]

Just six days after Sgt Gilroy had been killed another Darlington airman serving with 431 Squadron also lost his life on operations.

On the night of 28/29 January Harris once again tried to attack the German capital. 677 aircraft took part in what was a reasonably successful raid. Some German fighters were decoyed away but losses over Berlin itself were high and a total of 46 aircraft failed to return. 431 Squadron suffered heavily on the night, losing four aircraft. Amongst them was Halifax V (LL181, SE-Q). P/O W.R. Hewetson, RCAF, and his crew were all killed. The mid-upper gunner in the crew was Sgt George Frederick Carter, a 20-years-old Darlington lad.[33]

The sorry toll of Darlington men who had lost their lives training to fly heavy bombers continued to rise and on 7 February trainee navigator Sergeant Kenneth Murray (23) joined the roll of honour. Sergeant Murray had taken off aboard Halifax II (BB320, -A2) from RAF Lindholme, where he was based with 1665 Heavy Conversion Unit (HCU), for a night navigational detail. Just fifty minutes into the flight the Halifax was observed coming out of cloud in a spin and it crashed at 6.30pm on Kingsley Moor near Cheadle, killing all six of the men aboard.[34]

Yet another Darlington airman was killed in an accidental crash on 23 February. Flying Officer Frederick Jones was a 20-year-old navigator with 236 Squadron of Coastal Command. 236 Squadron was part of the North Coates Strike Wing which mounted anti-shipping patrols. On the day in question he and his pilot, Flying Officer Robert Barr, had taken off in Beaufighter TF.X (NE201, J), but the aircraft crashed into the sea shortly after take-off killing both of the crew.[35] Demonstrating the loss and anguish experienced by those parents who lost sons during the war, Flying Officer Jones' parents, Frederick and Mildred, had the following inscription placed upon their son's headstone: THINK OF HIM STILL AS THE SAME, WE SAY HE IS NOT DEAD HE IS JUST AWAY.

On the same day that Flying Officer Jones lost his life another Darlington airman was also killed. Sergeant Francis Robert Simmons, aged 22, was part of the crew of Wellington IX (MP643) of 38 Squadron based in Greece as part of 201 Group flying shipping interdiction operations including minelaying, reconnaissance and anti-submarine duties. On 23 February Sergeant Simmons and his crew were detailed for an anti-shipping operation over the Aegean sea, but nothing further was heard and the Wellington failed to return.[36]

The casualties suffered among Darlington men who were flying with Bomber Command continued in February. On the night of 25/26 February the majority of the command were sent to bomb Augsburg, but there was also a major minelaying effort mounted as a diversion. Known to the crews as gardening (with the mines referred to as vegetables) these sorties were seen as being reasonably easy but there was still a steady stream of casualties from these operations. When these operations were used as diversions, they often involved crews or squadrons flying obsolescent aircraft. 102 Squadron at RAF Pocklington in the East Riding of Yorkshire was still struggling along with the obsolescent earlier marks of the Halifax. On this night the crew of Flight Sergeant S.J. Rogers, RCAF, took off at 8.12pm for mining operations over the Baltic. The Halifax II (LW331, DY-D), for unknown reasons, came down in the North Sea off Bridlington and, despite an extensive search and rescue operation, no trace of the Halifax or its crew was ever found. The wireless operator/air gunner aboard the Halifax was a very experienced airman from Darlington. Flight Lieutenant Thomas Leithead, DFM, was a 29-year-old married man who had been born at Hawick in the Scottish Borders. Before enlisting he had worked at the Royal Bank of Scotland in St Boswells and had played rugby for Melrose RFC. He had been awarded his DFM on 26 June 1942 for his efforts while serving with 51 Squadron when he had been instrumental in guiding his damaged Whitley bomber back from an operation to Frankfurt in October 1941. Although his personal connections with Darlington were limited, it seems his parents were living there in 1944 and were notified of his death at their home there. At the time of his death he was serving as 102 Squadron's Signals Leader.[37]

March continued to take its toll of Darlington's trainee airmen when Sgt Ernest Small (20) was killed in a crash while based at 28 OTU at

RAF Castle Donington. He and his crew, under pilot F/Sgt A.J. Mosley, RAAF, took off at 11:19 pm on the night of 16 March but crashed within a minute of becoming airborne. A subsequent inquiry established that the flaps on their Wellington IC (R1183) had dropped down while at just 200 feet. This gave the pilot no chance to recover and the Wellington stalled and crashed. The wireless operator was killed in the crash and Sgt Small died of his injuries the next day.

On the night of 18/19 March, and with Arthur Harris being increasingly aware that his command would shortly be required to switch targets to aid in the build-up to D-Day, an operation to attack Frankfurt with 846 aircraft was planned. Extensive diversionary mining operations again took place and successfully split the German night fighter force. The raid was a great success, resulting in heavy damage to the city for the loss of only 22 aircraft. Amongst the losses, however, was yet another Darlington airman. Lancaster III (ND596, CF-H) of 625 Squadron took off from RAF Kestern at 7:08 pm but nothing more was heard from the crew of F/O I.E. MacMaster and they were declared missing. The Lancaster had indeed been shot down and only the flight engineer survived. Sgt Alan Wood (20) was the navigator in the crew and, like the rest of the crew, is buried at Durnbach War Cemetery.

Three days after the death of Sgt Wood, the people of Darlington suffered further loss when Sgt Ronald Thorpe (29) lost his life in yet another training accident. Based at 1658 HCU at RAF Riccall, the crew of Halifax II ((W7865) took off for a general training flight with P/O P.T. Bath, RCAF, at the controls but the bomber crashed shortly before 6 pm on the York-Knaresborough railway line at the village of Kirk Hammerton. The pilot was killed in the crash and the rest of the crew injured. Sgt Thorpe, the rear air gunner, was taken to RAF Rufforth's sick quarters where he succumbed to his injuries. Sgt Thorpe was a Richmond man, but he had married a Darlington woman, Louvaine Thorpe.[38]

A further training accident claimed the life of yet another Darlington airman on the night of 27 March when air gunner Sergeant Thomas Longstaff was killed while serving with 14 OTU. Sergeant Longstaff and his crew, under the command of Flight Sergeant E.K. Ferguson, RAAF, took off at 8.49pm from RAF Husbands Bosworth aboard Wellington IC (R1669) for night circuits and landings practice. A couple of hours later the Wellington was approaching the runway when it swung and dived into the ground close to the airfield perimeter. The bomber exploded and caught fire on impact and all six of the crew were killed. The Wellington in which the crew lost their lives had been accepted on charge in July 1943 and had amassed over 1,200 flying hours during its career (spent solely with OTUs). It was the last Wellington IC to be lost by 14 OTU.[39]

On 30/31 March there was almost a full moon and the majority of Bomber Command airmen expected, as was usual in such conditions, to be stood-down. Instead, they found themselves being briefed for a deep-penetration raid into southern Germany to attack Nuremburg. Harris was taking this risk, despite the concerns of some of his officers, as it was the last real chance for a mass raid on a city target before his command was switched to targets in advance of D-Day. The raid was a disaster. The straight-in route took the bombers close to a fighter assembly beacon, weather conditions were against the bombers and casualties to night fighters were extremely high with ninety-five bombers being lost and bombing results very poor. 103 Squadron at Elsham Wolds, Lincs, lost two Lancasters on the raid. The bomb-aimer in one of the bombers was from Darlington. Sergeant Edwin McCully was aged just 21 when he lost his life while flying with the crew of Pilot Officer R.R.J. Tate when their Lancaster was shot down by a night fighter on the outbound route to Nuremburg.[40]

One of the many useful tasks in which RAF Bomber Command participated was the supply of equipment to the resistance movements in Europe on behalf of the Special Operations Executive (SOE). These flights were extremely dangerous being made alone and often at relatively low-level. One of the squadrons which took part in these operations was 620 Squadron which was based at RAF Fairford.

The squadron was part of 38 Group and was practised at parachute drops as it had been training to take part in the D-Day landings. With the approaching invasion, efforts to provide supplies to the French resistance stepped up. On the night of 7/8 May 1944 the crew of Stirling IV (LJ886) was briefed to drop supplies over France but the Stirling failed to return from the operation and it was later established that it had been shot down near Poisson. The navigator in the crew was a married Darlington airman, 27-year-old Flight Sergeant James Henry Bennison Lister.[41]

Yet another Darlington airman lost his life in a training exercise in the early hours of 16 May. The aircraft involved was Lancaster X (KB701, VR-B) of 419 (Moose) Squadron, RCAF, based at RAF Middleton St George. F/O J.G. McMaster, RCAF, was the pilot of the crew but at 3:40 am the Lancaster crashed at Potter House Farm near Wombleton. All of the crew were killed in the crash. Like many the largely RCAF crew had a British flight engineer but it was one of the RCAF crew who was from Darlington. Sgt Norman Frederick Alsop (20), RCAF, was Darlington-born but, like many young British men, had emigrated to Canada.

On 17 May 1944 another Darlington man lost his life in his country's service. Flying Officer Norman Liddle (20) was part of a trainee crew which was detailed to take part in a navigational exercise under the tutelage of a screened navigator instructor and with two trainee pilots (including their own). The Wellington X (MP314) took off from RAF Bruntingthorpe in Leicestershire at 11.25am and was seen coming out of cloud in a steep dive from which it failed to recover, crashing at 12.15pm at Mendham, killing all aboard.[42]

Yet another Darlington family suffered the loss of a loved one when Carl and Nellie Warburton received the news that their son had failed to return from operations over Germany. Sgt Carl Arthur Warburton was the wireless operator in a 75 Squadron Lancaster which was one of 361 Lancasters and 14 Mosquitoes sent to bomb Dortmund on the night of 22/23 May; an attack which cost eighteen Lancasters. P/O

C.E. Armstrong, RNZAF, was also among the crew. Their Lancaster III (ND768, AA-F) had been hit by flak which caused the bomb load to detonate, killing the entire crew instantly.[43]

With the campaign in Normandy continuing, Bomber Command was increasingly used in a tactical role against precision targets. The accuracy of the Command surprised even those in charge. Many of the raids in this period were targeted against the railway network in France (others were targeted against flying bomb sites) and on the night of 27/28 June a combined force of 214 Lancasters and nine Mosquitoes was sent to bomb railway yards at Vaires and at Vitry. Only four Lancasters were lost during the operation, but one of them contained yet another Darlington airman. Sergeant Jack Desmond Pepper was born in Newton Aycliffe and was just 19-years of age when he was killed while serving as wireless operator in the 106 Squadron crew of Flight Sergeant E.C. Fox.[44]

As we have already heard the period in the aftermath of the D-Day landings was an exceptionally busy one for the men of Bomber Command. Although their targets were now more often in France rather than heavily-defended Germany the operations were still exceptionally dangerous and the fact that the authorities had decreed that sorties over France would only count as one-third of an operation caused a great deal of resentment. Many of the operations launched during the period were against sites related to the flying bombs which were raining down in London and the south-east. On the night of 7/8 July 208 Lancasters and 13 Mosquitoes from 5 and 8 Groups attacked a flying bomb storage site at St-Leu-D'Esserent. The bombing was successful but German night fighters intercepted the force and 29 Lancasters and two Mosquitoes were shot down as a result (a loss of fourteen per cent). At RAF Metheringham, 106 Squadron had dispatched sixteen Lancasters on the operation but only eleven returned. Several other squadrons lost multiple aircraft. 44 Squadron at RAF Dunholme Lodge lost three of its aircraft. Lancaster I (ME859, KM-S) had taken off at 10:33 pm under the command of P/O D. Graaf but failed to return. The navigator was 22-years-old F/O Victor Davenant Purvis, DFC. F/O Purvis had been born in Gateshead but lived at Darlington with his parents and had flown on many operational sorties to Germany and Italy. He was highly rated for his navigational skills and was navigation leader on the squadron. His DFC had been gazetted on 4 February 1944.[45]

On the same day that F/O Purvis was killed another Darlington airman was killed. F/Sgt Ronald Wilfred Taylor was a 22-years-old Spitfire pilot with 249 Squadron. The squadron was based in Italy and was flying fighter-bomber operations over Albania and Yugoslavia. This involved dive-bombing and this dangerous technique had to be constantly practised. It was during such a practice flight that

Flying Officer Victor Davenant Purvis, DFC. (Unknown)

F/Sgt Taylor was killed when his Spitfire VC (JK929) failed to recover from a dive over the airfield.[46]

On the night of 20/21 July 1944 Bomber Command mounted attacks on two oil targets in Germany and on railway targets at Courtrai in Belgium. The Courtrai force consisted of 302 Lancasters and fifteen Mosquitoes drawn from 1, 5, and 8 Groups, and their target was the railway yards and a triangle rail junction. The attack was a huge success with assessments claiming that the targets were both devastated. Nine of the Lancasters failed to return.

Among them was Lancaster III (D654, AR-R) of 460 (RAAF) Squadron which had taken off from RAF Binbrook in Lincolnshire at 12.14am to attack the railway yards. The Lancaster was shot down and crashed at Poelkapelle in Belgium at 1.30am. The flight engineer in the crew was 24-year-old Sergeant Kenneth G. Butler from Darlington, where he lived with his mother at West Auckland Road. Before the war he had been a railway fitter. His mother received a telegram shortly afterwards, notifying her that her son was missing following operations. For Mrs Butler this must have been a terrible blow, made even worse by the fact that his younger brother had been killed in action two years previously. In this case, however, there was a happy ending when, in late September, Sergeant Butler arrived back in Britain safe and well. The seven-man crew had baled out of the stricken Lancaster and six of them had been hidden for two months by members of the French resistance before being returned to Allied lines.[47]

As we have previously seen the V-Weapon attacks had caused disruption in Darlington but the attacks claimed a Darlington victim on 2 August when a bomb dropped on Lorne Gardens, Shirley, Croydon. This was the marital home of 37-year-old Flight Lieutenant William Henry Burt and his 40-year-old wife Edith Annie (née Thompson). Both were killed in the subsequent explosion. F/Lt Burt had grown up at Thornton Street, Darlington, while his wife was from Middlesbrough. F/Lt Burt had been educated at Bondgate Street School and the Technical College before going on to a career as an inspector for Imperial Airways and transferred to the RAF at the beginning of the war. He was employed in the RAF as an inspector of crashed aircraft and travelled widely across the country as part of his duties but was at home on leave at the time of his death.[48]

The night of 18/19 August saw Bomber Command launch raids against multiple targets. Mid-upper gunner W/O Arthur Thomas Raine was killed with his crew when their 635 Lancaster VI (JB713, F2-Z) failed to return from a sortie to Harburg. W/O Raine was a resident of the attractive Darlington suburb of Cockerton and was aged 24 at the time of his death; he had been an orphan who had been adopted by James and Sarah Wood. He was a married man and left behind his widow, Edith, in Cockerton. W/O Raine was an experienced gunner who had joined the RAF in the first months of the war and had previously flown a tour of operation on the Halifaxes of 102 Squadron. During this tour he had a lucky escape when he escaped a crash landing near Huby on 4 January 1943.[49]

Finally, on the last day of August, Sergeant James Lambell, a trainee navigator with 1654 HCU, was killed along with his crew when their Stirling III (LJ639) crashed. The Stirling had taken off at 11.25pm on what was described as a lengthy cross-country navigational exercise, but crashed just twenty-five minutes later following a reported fire in one of its starboard engines. Sergeant Lambell was a married man and, aged 36, was older than most aircrew.[50]

As the year wore on the airmen of Bomber Command found themselves once again attacking targets in Germany rather than those in France in support of the invasion. On the night of 19/20 October Bomber Command operations included an attack on Stuttgart made by 565 Lancasters and eighteen Mosquitoes drawn from 1, 3, 6, and 8 Groups. The attack was made in two waves and caused serious damage for the loss of just six Lancasters. Among the losses was one Lancaster from 186 Squadron. This squadron had only formed on 4 October and during the course of the war suffered just thirteen losses during the war (four in 1944 and nine in 1945). The loss of the Lancaster on the Stuttgart operation included the loss of two men from Darlington. The flight engineer and navigator aboard Lancaster I (NG176, AP-H) were both from the town and were killed with the rest of their crew when the bomber came down at Andilly, France. Both of the Darlington men were aged 22. The flight engineer was Sergeant Edward Brunskill while the navigator was Sergeant William Raine.[51]

November 1944 proved to be a particularly tragic one for Darlington airmen with at least four airmen with connections to the town losing their lives, three of them on the same date. With RAF Fighter Command increasingly operating from bases which had been captured in occupied Europe following the invasion, there was a need for ever-increasing numbers of personnel to operate from these newly established bases. It was not just Fighter Command, the aircraft of Bomber Command often relied on radar to bomb accurately and radar stations were being built in Europe to facilitate this. On 7 November there was a tragedy which resulted in the death of a Darlington RAF man. Sergeant Maurice Sedgwick was a 33-year-old married man serving with the Base Signals and Radar Unit (BSRU) and was being transferred to France aboard Landing Ship Tank (LST) 420. The weather became poor when off Ostend, and the captain decided to return to Dover. Shortly after turning around the LST struck a mine and sank. There were only thirty-one survivors with fourteen officers and 224 other ranks being killed.[52]

On 11 November, 22-year-old Flying Officer William Derringham Hodgson was assigned to 75 OTU at Gianaclis, Egypt. On the night of 11 November he was detailed for a night sortie in Baltimore I (FW812) but the aircraft crashed shortly after take-off and Flying Officer Hodgson was killed. We have already seen an example of two Darlington men being killed while serving as part of the same crew in a Bomber Command aircraft. On the night of 11/12 November the command dispatched 237 Lancasters and eight Mosquitoes to attack the Rhenania-Ossag oil refinery at Harburg. One of the seven Lancasters lost on this sortie was Lancaster III (PB356, PG-G) of 619 Squadron. The crew was flying with a second-dickie pilot on the operation, but the bomber failed to return and the crew were reported missing believed killed. The two air gunners in the crew of Flying Officer P.C. Clapham were both from Darlington: 30-years-old Sergeant George Nixon was the mid-upper gunner while 29-years-old Sergeant Reginald Patterson was the rear gunner. Only three bodies were recovered, those of the flight engineer and both gunners. It is fitting that the two Darlington air gunners lie together at Hamburg Cemetery.

Just days after these deaths, another Darlington airman lost his life in a tragic accident while returning home. At this point in the war many

RAF personnel were being transferred from the Middle East back to Britain. On 14 November, Liberator II (AL584) of 144 MU of Middle East Command was caught in a snowstorm on its way back over France and flew into a mountain near Autun. All eight crew and passengers were killed. The dead included Flight Sergeant William David Smith, the 26-year-old son of the Reverend William Edward Smith and Catherine Smith of Darlington. Flight Sergeant Smith and the rest of those killed in the tragic accident are buried at Choloy War Cemetery in France where Flight Sergeant Smith's family, presumably his siblings, had the following inscribed upon his headstone: GOD BLESS OUR HERO. BETTY, PETER AND MARGOT.

Late December also brought further tragedy and loss to those Darlington families with loved ones in Bomber Command. Many of the Darlington airmen who were killed while flying with the command were not pilots but were employed in other aircrew trades but a Darlington bomber pilot did lose his life in the early hours of 22 December. Bomber Command was now so powerful that it could send raids to several targets in one night. On this night the main target was a synthetic-oil refinery at Politz near Stettin, an extremely distant target. The operation was solely the province of 5 Group which now had its own target-marking force and was acting semi-independently of the rest of the force. Three Lancasters were lost with a further three crashing upon return to Britain as a result of fog at some airfields and low fuel after the lengthy flight. One of the aircraft which crashed upon return was Lancaster I (NG258) from 630 Squadron. The Lancaster had taken off from RAF East Kirkby at 4:58 pm but crashed at 2:50 am at Scanfield Farm. The pilot, F/O Arnold Stockill (31) and five of his crew were killed while the gunner was injured. F/O Stockill's widow and family had his body brought home for cremation at Darlington Crematorium.

On the night following the death of F/O Stockill Bomber Command sent 106 aircraft, mainly Halifaxes from 4 Group, to attack the railway yards at Bingen. The attack was highly accurate and only three aircraft were lost. Amongst them was Halifax III (NA501, LK-X) of 578 Squadron at RAF Burn. The Halifax had bombed and was homebound at 15,000 feet when a Ju88 night fighter shot it down. Five of the crew survived, four as PoWs and one who managed to evade capture, but two of the three air gunners were killed. The mid-upper air gunner was F/Sgt Gordon Stewart, a Darlington native.[53]

1945

As we have seen, the families of many men posted missing often had to wait some time before the fate of their loved one was confirmed. Sgt Thomas Tiffin Elliott, a 35-years-old married flight engineer from Darlington, was posted missing after failing to return from an operation to Chemnitz on the night of 5/6 March while serving with 10 Squadron. It was later confirmed that Halifax III (NR131, ZA-N), piloted by F/Lt A.D. Stephen, had crashed near to Stalag IXC at Mulhausen. The bodies of the seven crew were recovered from the wreckage but the local commander ordered that there should be no formal burial service. Despite this, a PoW, the Reverend J.R. Bamber, conducted a ceremony two weeks after the men had lost their lives.[54] It was not until August 1945, after the war in Europe had ended, that Sgt Elliot's wife received confirmation of her husband's death.

Endnotes

Chapter 1

1. It was reported a year later that a young girl had drowned in one of the craters left on this night.
2. *Middlesbrough Daily Gazette*, 23rd May 1940, p. 6.
3. *Newcastle Journal*, 30 August 1941, p. 1.
4. *Newcastle Journal*, 2 June 1944, p. 4.
5. *Newcastle Journal*, 13 April 1944, p. 4.

Chapter 2

1. Both Signalman Case and Hinnigan are buried at Darlington West Cemetery while Signalman Treslove lies in Darlington North Cemetery.
2. *Daily Gazette for Middlesbrough*, 7 September 1939, p. 3.
3. *Daily Gazette for Middlesbrough*, 19 September 1939, p. 3.
4. *Daily Gazette for Middlesbrough*, 26 September 1939, p. 3.
5. *Daily Gazette for Middlesbrough*, 26 October 1939, p. 3.
6. *Newcastle Evening Chronicle*, 1 January 1940, p. 7.
7. Gunner Leonard was from School House, Coxlodge, Newcastle-upon-Tyne, and is buried at Ashburton Roman Catholic Cemetery, Gosforth.
8. *Newcastle Journal*, 7 March 1940, p. 12.
9. The second man was a Newcastle banker named Mr Michael F. Mounsey.
10. *Newcastle Journal*, 7 March 1941, p. 5.
11. *Newcastle Journal*, 11 September 1941, p. 3.

12. *Hartlepool Daily Mail*, 22 December 1944, p. 8.

13. The money was used to fund the endowment of two children's cots in Darlington Memorial Hospital. Plaques with the names of contributors were affixed above the cots but only one now survives in the entrance to the hospital.

14. A cairn was later erected at the site of the crash and a street in the town named McMullen Road. Pilot Officer McMullen rests in Harrogate (Stonefall) Cemetery.

15. Hardman had become the first Socialist President of the Cambridge Union in 1924 but remained as MP for Darlington for only six years before being defeated by the Conservative candidate in the 1951 election.

Chapter 3

1. Parts of the crashed bomber were on display at the North East Aviation Museum.

Chapter 4

1. Sergeant John Frederick Knightson, 6th Gordon Highlanders, was killed in action aged 31 on 3 April 1944 during the fighting at Anzio. He is buried at the Beach Head War Cemetery.

2. *Newcastle Journal*, 5 April 1940, p. 3.

3. *Yorkshire Post and Leeds Intelligencer*, 17 May 1940, p. 8.

4. *Newcastle Journal*, 4 October 1940, p. 5.

5. *Newcastle Journal*, 22 July 1943, p. 4.

6. *Newcastle Journal*, 3 March 1944, p. 4.

Chapter 5

1. *Daily Gazette for Middlesbrough*, 5 November 1940, p. 4.

Chapter 6

1. Henry Williams, Ltd was an engineering firm which specialised in permanent way and signalling engineering.
2. Kingaby was posted as an instructor to an OTU in Scotland and was very deservedly commissioned. He joined 64 Squadron in April 1942 where he scored a couple more victories before being promoted to Flight Lieutenant and posted to 122 Squadron as a flight commander. Shortly afterwards he was promoted to Squadron Leader and took over command of the squadron. During his time with 122 he scored more victories and was awarded the DSO. After a short rest period at Fighter Command HQ he was promoted to Wing Commander and took over the Hornchurch Wing in 1944. In the summer of 1944 he saw action over Normandy and scored his final victory (a shared claim over an Me109). He finished the war as Wing Commander Kingaby, DSO, DFM (and two Bars), and, with 22½ confirmed victories, was the 22nd highest ranking RAF ace of the war.
3. Struck off charge was the formal term for saying that the aircraft had been removed from the official operational RAF. In most cases it meant that the aircraft had been scrapped.

Chapter 7

1. This was the first Halifax to be lost on operations.
2. A later inspection of the wreckage found that the Halifax had probably been damaged by enemy action.
3. Beam Approach Training Flights were units which allowed pilots to practise making blind approaches to runways using wireless and radar techniques.

Chapter 8

1. All three casualties from the *Royal Oak* are commemorated on the Portsmouth Naval Memorial.

2. Able Seaman Bulmer was reportedly buried at sea and he is commemorated on the Chatham Naval Memorial. HMS *Curacoa* went on to be sunk after she collided with the RMS *Queen Mary* on 2 October 1942.

3. HMS *Liverpool* was repaired and served until the late 1950s, surviving being torpedoed once more in 1942.

4. There is some confusion over both the date and the facts surrounding the loss of HMS *Triad* with the CWGC giving the date of death as 20 October but most other sources placing the sinking of the submarine on 15 October.

5. Ordinary Seaman Jackson is commemorated on the Portsmouth Naval Memorial.

6. Ordinary Seaman Oldfield is commemorated on the Plymouth Naval Memorial.

7. Seaman Rea is commemorated on the Lowestoft Naval Memorial. The author's grandfather, Skipper Robert Armstrong, served as captain of a sister ship, the HMS *Derby County*.

8. Able Seaman Johnson is commemorated on the Portsmouth Naval Memorial. The loss of 147 lives was the greatest loss of life on any ship off the east coast during the war. The wreckage of HMS *Vortigern* proved a serious hazard to navigation and she was broken up with explosives, although the site is still designated as a war grave.

9. Chief Engine Room Artificer Longbone is commemorated on the Chatham Naval Memorial.

10. Able Seaman Bath is commemorated on the Portsmouth Naval Memorial. HMS *Marne* was repaired and after the war was transferred to the Turkish Navy, in which she served until 1970.

11. Lieutenant Maw is commemorated on the Portsmouth Naval Memorial. The CWGC has his date of death listed as 28 March but this seems to be an error.

12. Both men are commemorated on the Portsmouth Naval Memorial.

Chapter 9

1. Driver Slater is buried at Darlington West Cemetery.
2. All three Darlington Privates are buried at Nord-Sel Churchyard.
3. There are only nine Second World War burials at Wervicq, one of them unidentified.
4. The bodies of thirty-three of the victims were washed up on the coast of Co Donegal over the next fortnight.
5. Signalman Howard lies in Darlington East Cemetery.
6. Lance Corporal John Vincent McDonald, 6th Heavy Anti-Aircraft Regiment, Royal Artillery Signal Section, Royal Corps of Signals, is commemorated on the Singapore Memorial.
7. Gunner Trevena lies in Bone War Cemetery, Annaba.
8. Lance Corporal Snailham is amongst the 1,956 Allied casualties who have no known graves and are commemorated on the Medjez-al-Bab Memorial.
9. Gunner Dye is commemorated on the Singapore Memorial.
10. Lieutenant McGilvray is buried at Sfax War Cemetery. On 12 April 1944 his mother placed the following in the *Kirkintilloch Herald*, 'My eyes grow dim with tenderness awhile thinking I hear you: thinking I see you smile: remembered, John.
11. The Brookwood Memorial is dedicated to the memory of nearly 3,500 men and women of the Commonwealth land forces who died during the war, have no known graves, and could not be appropriately commemorated on any of the other campaign memorials.
12. Private Bland is buried at Salerno War Cemetery.
13. Trooper Schott is buried at Minturno War Cemetery.
14. Lance Sergeant Fenwick and Sapper Walker are buried at Hermanville War Cemetery in the village of the same name behind Sword Beach. Sapper Lockhart has no known grave and is commemorated on the Bayeux Memorial. Private Redding is buried at the Bayeux War Cemetery.

Chapter 10

1. AC2 Squires is buried in Darlington West Cemetery.
2. AC1 Greenall is buried at Darlington North Cemetery.
3. Sergeant Colling is buried at Fouquieres Churchyard Extension. The remaining crew were: Sergeant C.C. Bennett, RAF (pilot); and Aircraftman 2nd Class (AC2) E. Hannah, RAF (wireless operator/ air gunner).
4. Sergeant Wigham is buried at Darlington West Cemetery.
5. All three crew were killed. Sergeant Bartlett is buried at The Hague (Westduin) General Cemetery.
6. F/Sgt Ward is buried at Hamburg Cemetery.
7. Sgt Bell is buried at Barrie Union Cemetery, Ontario.
8. F/Lt Bell is buried at Durnbach War Cemetery.
9. F/Sgt Dormand is buried at the Reichswald Forest War Cemetery.
10. The crew were: P/O J.A. Worswick, DFC, RAF (pilot); Sgt R.I. Hart, RAF (flight engineer); W/O G. Robson, DFM, RAF (navigator); P/O A.G. Bake, DFM, RAF (bomb-aimer); Sgt J.D. Brown, RAF (wireless-operator); Sgt T.E. Hodgson, RAF (air gunner); and Sgt W.L. Lambert, RAF (air gunner). All are buried at Reichswald Forest War Cemetery.
11. F/Sgt Metcalfe and his pilot have no known graves and are commemorated on the Runnymede Memorial.
12. [N]ational [A]rchives: AIR 81/ 727 (P 352618/40). F/O H.P Dixon.
13. Sgt Scotland and his pilot are buried at Schoonselhof Cemetery.
14. Sq/Ldr W. Clarker, RAF (pilot); Sgt G.E. Johnson, RAF (navigator); and Sgt J.C. Adam, RAF (air gunner) were killed and are buried at Benschop General Cemetery.
15. Sgt Siddell is buried at Hartlepool (Stranton) Cemetery. The tutor pilot, F/Lt Marriott, DFM, had flown a tour of bombing operations with 115 Squadron at the beginning of the war and had been awarded his DFM in March 1941.

16. Sgt Graham and the rest of the casualties are commemorated on the Malta Memorial.

17. Halifax JB867 lived something of a cursed life. Built by English Electric at Samlesbury and taken on charge by 102 Squadron on 18 March 1943. The aircraft suffered minor flak damage on 30 March 1943, was again damaged on the occasion when F/O McLoughlin was killed, and then on 5 May 1943 it crashed on take-off for a training flight and was damaged beyond repair. At the time it was struck off charge on 16 May it had flown just 53 hours. The pilot on this last flight was a F/O A. Gibson, none of the crew were injured.

18. F/O Lupton is commemorated on the Runnymede Memorial along with his wireless operator, Sgt W.F. Whitfield, RAF, and his bomb-aimer, Sgt J.P. Metton, RCAF. Sgt Merton had survived the initial impact but died shortly afterwards. The two survivors, F/O R.A. Lord, RAF (navigator) and F/O E.G. Hadingham (air gunner), were picked up and returned to Britain, exhausted but uninjured.

19. Sgt Harker is buried at Darlington West Cemetery. Sgt Richmond and his crew had experienced a lucky escape just a fortnight earlier when a propellor fell off their aircraft on take-off.

20. Sgt Butler is buried at Tripoli War Cemetery.

21. The dead crew were: Sgt D.McN. Thomson, RAAF (pilot); Sgt J.L. Osborne, RAF (flight engineer); Sgt K. Bowes, RAF (navigator); Sgt W.M. Ward, RAF (bomb-aimer); and Sgt D.N. Campbell, RAF (wireless operator/air gunner). The dead, barring Sgt Bowes, are buried at New Eastern Cemetery, Amsterdam. The survivors were both RCAF air gunners: Sgt W.T. Pingle and Sgt C.W.A. Sparling. A propellor from the Lancaster was recovered and now stands in front of the town hall at Dronten. An air gunners' parade is held here every year. The loss of five aircraft in a single night was the worst loss suffered by 12 Squadron in the whole of 1943.

22. The crew were: Sgt G.C. Parritt, RAF (pilot); Sgt J.L. Burnside, RAF (flight engineer); Sgt L. Harris, RAF (navigator); Sgt B.L.

Howard, RAF (bomb-aimer); Sgt R.E. Archer, RAF (wireless operator/air gunner); Sgt C.G.L. Vallance, RAF (air gunner); and Sgt R.J. Coggins, RAF (air gunner). All are buried at Heverlee War Cemetery.

23. The crew were: Sgt W. Dench, RAF (pilot); P/O H.E. Kessop-Philip, RAF (navigator); Sgt J. Richardson, RAF (wireless operator/air gunner); P/O R.J. Herbert, RAF (bomb-aimer); and W/O2 M.G. Petz, RCAF (air gunner). W/O2 Petz is buried at Agira Canadian War Cemetery while the others are buried at Catania War Cemetery.

24. The crew were: F/O I.D.C. Evans, RAF (pilot); P/O A.P. Reed, RAAF (second pilot); P/O S.C. Sykes, RAF (navigator); F/O L.H. Burn, RAF (wireless operator/air gunner); F/O N. Avery, RAF (-aimer); and F/O D.B. Surrette, RCAF (air gunner). All were killed and are commemorated on the Mata Memorial.

25. The crew were: P/.O G.V. Helm, RNZAF (pilot); Sgt O. McCoo, RAF (flight engineer); F/Sgt D.M. Stewart, RNZAF (navigator); F/Sgt J.G.A. Fisk, RNZAF (bomb-aimer); Sgt A.J. Bishop, RAF (wireless operator/air gunner); Sgt G.T. Burglass, Raf (air gunner); and Sgt F.T.J. Harries, RAF (air gunner). The dead are buried at Berlin 1939-1945 War Cemetery.

26. The crew consisted of: F/O A.F. Bremner, RAF (pilot); Sgt R.M. Appleton, RAF (flight engineer); F/Sgt R.R. Woodhouse, RAF (navigator); F/Sgt A.D. Archer, RAF (bomb aimer); Sgt J.H.V. Horsley, RAF (wireless operator/air gunner); Sgt A.E. Smith, RAF (air gunner); and F/Sgt F.W. Dyde, RAF (air gunner). The bodies of the pilot and both air gunners were identified but the remaining crew are commemorated on the Runnymede Memorial.

27. The crew were: P/O W.A. Clark, RAF (pilot); Sgt G.A. Crowe, RAF (flight engineer); Sgt R.H. Banks, RAF (navigator); F/O L.R. Rinn, RCAF (bomb-aimer); Sgt J. Ford, RAF (wireless operator/ air gunner); Sgt R. Hughes, RAF (air gunner); and F/Sgt C.R. McLaren, RAAF (air gunner). They are all buried at the Berlin 1939-1945 War Cemetery.

28. Those who died were all RAF men: Sgt J.W. Hinde (pilot); Sgt D.F. Faulkner (flight engineer); Sgt W.J. Bellinger (navigator); F/O H. Clark (bomb aimer); Sgt A.W. Watson (air gunner); and Sgt D.F. Butler. The survivor was F/Sgt C.H.T. Hurley (wireless operator/air gunner). It was only a temporary reprieve for Hurley. On 21/22 June 1944, and still serving with 57 Squadron, the now W/O Hurley was part of the crew of F/Lt R.A. Beaumont, tasked as one of 133 Lancasters and six Mosquitoes sent to attack a synthetic oil plant at Wesseling. The raid was a disaster with little damage being done and 37 Lancasters being shot down by enemy night fighters. Amongst them was that of F/Lt Beaumont. All seven of the crew were killed. W/O Hurley is commemorated on the Runnymede Memorial.

29. The crew were: F/Sgt H.R.H. Ross, RAAF (pilot); Sgt F.G. Clark, RAF (flight engineer); F/Lt A. Walker, RAF (navigator); Sgt H.D.G. Aldiss, RAF (bomb-aimer); Sgt H.R. McDowell, RAAF (wireless operator/air gunner); Sgt A.T. Broome, RAF (air gunner); and Sgt R.A. Whitley, RAF (air gunner). The two Australian crew members were buried at Cambridge City Cemetery. F/Lt Walker is buried at Whitehaven Cemetery.

30. The crew consisted of: F/Sgt A. Molloy, RAAF (pilot); Sgt A.D. Meynell, RAF (flight engineer); Sgt F.E.J. Hothersall, RNZAF (navigator); F/O B.D. Heading, RAAF (bomb aimer); F/Sgt F.W. Doonan, RAAF (wireless operator/air gunner); Sgt W.E. Edwards, RCAF (air gunner); and Sgt J.M. Blake, RCAF (air gunner). Apart from Sgt Meynell they are buried in Harrogate (Stonefall) Cemetery.

31. Sq/Ldr Moore was a Battle of Britain veteran. He had joined the RAF in 1937 and flew Bristol Blenheims with 236 Squadron throughout the Battle.

32. Sgt Gilroy and the crewmen who were killed are buried at Becklingen War Cemetery.

33. Sgt Carter and his crew are buried at Berlin 1939-1945 War Cemetery.

34. Sgt Murray is buried at Darlington West Cemetery.

35. F/O Jones is buried at Darlington West Cemetery.

36. Sgt Simmons is commemorated on the Alamein Memorial.

37. F/Lt Leithead, DFM, and his crew are commemorated on the Runnymede Memorial.

38. Sgt Thorpe is buried at Richmond Cemetery. The other fatality amongst the crew was a passenger, P/O A.J. Coghill, who was a part of the flying control team at RAF Riccall.

39. Sgt Longstaff was buried at Ingleton (St John) Churchyard (in the Yorkshire Dales), one of just two CWGC burials there. A Darlington man, Sgt Longstaff had married a woman from Willington Quay, North Shields, Northumberland, Margaret Ann.

40. The crew were: P/O R.R.J. Tate, RAF (pilot); Sgt R.J. MacDonald, RAF (flight engineer); F/Sgt A.C. Belyea, RCAF (navigator); Sgt A.C. McCully, RAF (bomb-aimer); Sgt W.V. Ford, RAF (wireless operator/air gunner); Sgt J. Norgrove, RAF (air gunner); and Sgt P.J. Lynch, RAF (air gunner). The crew are buried in Hannover War Cemetery.

41. Sgt Lister and his crew are buried at Lyon (La Doua) French National Cemetery.

42. F/O Liddle is buried at Darlington West Cemetery.

43. Sgt Warburton and his crew are buried at the Reichswald Forest War Cemetery.

44. Sgt Pepper is buried at Dieppe Canadian War Cemetery.

45. F/O Purvis, DFC, and his crew lie in a communal grave at Equennes Churchyard, where they are the only CWGC burials.

46. F/Sgt Taylor is buried at Bari War Cemetery.

47. The mid-upper air gunner, Sgt R. Mills, RAF, was taken prisoner. The rest of the crew were: P/O R.H. Jopling, RAAF (pilot); Sgt K.G. Butler, RAF (flight engineer); Sgt J.G. Cawley, RCAF (navigator); F/Sgt R. Moffitt, RAAF (bomb-aimer); F/Sgt D.J. Annat, RAAF (wireless operator); F/Sgt L.G. Rosely, RAAF (rear air gunner). Although 460 Squadron was nominally an RAAF squadron

the crew demonstrates the mixed nature of crews even on these squadrons at this stage of the war with representatives from three air forces.

48. F/Lt Burt and his wife are buried at Shirley (St John) Churchyard.

49. W/O Raine and his crew are buried at Hamburg Cemetery. The Lancaster was one of just five which had been converted from a Mk III and was the only converted Mk VI Lancaster to be shot down during the war.

50. Sgt Lambell is buried at Thornley (St Helen) Churchyard in Nottinghamshire, where the crash occurred.

51. The crew, including both Darlington airmen, are buried at Choloy War Cemetery.

52. Sgt Sedgwick is commemorated on the Runnymede Memorial.

53. F/Sgt Stewart and his comrade are buried at Rheinberg War Cemetery.

54. Sgt Elliott and his crew are buried at the Berlin 1939-1945 War Cemetery.

Index